Skiing the North Shore

A guide to cross country trails in Minnesota's
spectacular Lake Superior region

ANDREW SLADE

Skiing the North Shore:
A guide to cross country trails in Minnesota's
spectacular Lake Superior region

Cover and book design: Sally Rauschenfels

Photography credits: cover © Getty Images; pgs. 24, 60, 77, 80, 89, 99, 114, 121,
125 © Corel Corporation; pgs. 30, 34, 48, 103, 118 © istockphoto Inc.;
p. 37 © Andrew Slade; p. 108 © Lutsen Resort; p. 139 © Superior National Forest

Although the author and publisher have researched all sources to ensure the
accuracy and completeness of the information contained in this book, we assume
no responsibility for errors, inaccuracies, omissions or any inconsistency herein.

ISBN 978-0-9794675-0-9

Library of Congress Control Number: 2007903316

Printed in the United States by Bang Printing.

First printing, June 2007

There & Back Books
1026 S. Lake Ave., Duluth, Minnesota 55802   Tel (218) 727-4873
www.thereandbackbooks.com

THERE AND
BACK BOOKS
READ. GO. DISCOVER.

This book is dedicated to the trail groomers,
who brave the dawn, fix the snow machines
and work for love or peanuts
so the we all can enjoy these trails.

Contents

Introduction...p.   8

DULUTH-SUPERIOR AREA: Urban Skiing Paradise

1   Jay Cooke State Park...p. 20
2   Superior Municipal Forest ....p. 25
3   Pattison State Park ....p. 28
4   Afterhours Ski Trail...p. 31
5   Magney Ski Area ....p. 35
6   Piedmont Ski Trail ....p. 38
7   Chester Bowl..p. 40
8   Hartley Field ....p. 42
9   Lester–Amity ....p. 45
10 Spirit Mountain..p. 49
11 Bagley Nature Area..p. 52
12 Snowflake Nordic Center ....p. 54
13 Boulder Lake ....p. 57
14 Canosia Wildlife Management Area Trail..............p. 61
15 Korkki Nordic Ski Center ....p. 64
16 Mother Bear Ski Trail...p. 67

LAKE COUNTY: Snow Country

17 Erkki Harju Ski Trail...p. 72
18 Gooseberry Falls State Park....................................p. 74
19 Split Rock Lighthouse State Park...........................p. 78
20 Northwoods Ski Touring Trail................................p. 81
21 Tettegouche State Park ....p. 84
22 Flathorn-Gegoka ....p. 87

NORTH SHORE MOUNTAINS: Everything is Connected

23	Sugarbush Trail System	p. 92
24	Lutsen Area	p. 104
25	Lutsen Mountains Nordic Center	p. 106
26	Solbakken Resort	p. 109
27	Cascade River State Park	p. 112
28	Cascade Lodge	p. 115
29	Deer Yard	p. 119
30	Bally Creek	p. 122

GUNFLINT TRAIL: Ski-In Hospitality

31	Pincushion Mountain	p. 128
32	George Washington Trail	p. 132
33	Central Gunflint	p. 134
34	Banadad Trail	p. 140
35	Upper Gunflint	p. 144

Resources for Planning your
North Shore Getaway

Resources for Planning your North Shore Getaway ... p. 150

Index ... p. 154

Foreword

I remember the day vividly. Crystal blue. Perfect tracks. Temperature in the upper 20s.

Half a dozen of us were rocking and rolling along the intimate Korkki Nordic ski trails between Duluth and Superior. We were classic skiing—the only kind of skiing you can do on these trails among the balsam fir and aging aspen.

The sun was making diamonds on the snow. The kick was good. The glide was better. I think all of us knew it might be the best day of skiing we would have all winter. Certainly, it would have been hard to top it.

I have no doubt that skiers all along the North Shore were having similar experiences on other trails. Up at the Erkki Harju Trail in Two Harbors. Along the North Shore Mountains Trails. Up at Pincushion on the hill above Grand Marais.

We are fortunate, here on the North Shore of Lake Superior, to have an amazing variety of cross country ski trails and, in most winters, plenty of snow to complement them. Most of us have our "home" trails, the ones that we can get to quickly for a spin before dark, or even a lighted loop that we can do after work.

But every now and then, we want to discover new country and different tracks. That's why this book by Andrew Slade is just what we need. We can keep it handy on the shelf at home or throw it in the daypack when we want to forge into new territory.

The maps and trail descriptions let us know exactly what we're getting into. Are the trails easy or difficult? Which loops are okay for the kids? What kind of views and scenery can we expect? How's the grooming likely to be? Is there a lodge or restaurant nearby?

Those are the questions we have when we venture onto new trails, and this book answers them.

But perhaps equally important, just looking at all of the trails waiting for us, we'll be inspired to get out and enjoy North Shore skiing even more than we already do.

Sam Cook
Duluth, Minnesota

Introduction

Minnesota's North Shore of Lake Superior is home to some of the best cross country skiing in North America.

A lucky bit of geology a billion years ago created the rugged topography of the Sawtooth Mountains. Then the glaciers of the last ice age created the world's largest freshwater lake. To this amazing landscape, add the legacy of 100 years of hospitality and ski trails built by the descendants of loggers and fishing families.

Today, with abundant snowfall from moisture off Lake Superior and over seven hundred kilometers of perfectly groomed ski trails, you'll find a world-class skiing experience like no other.

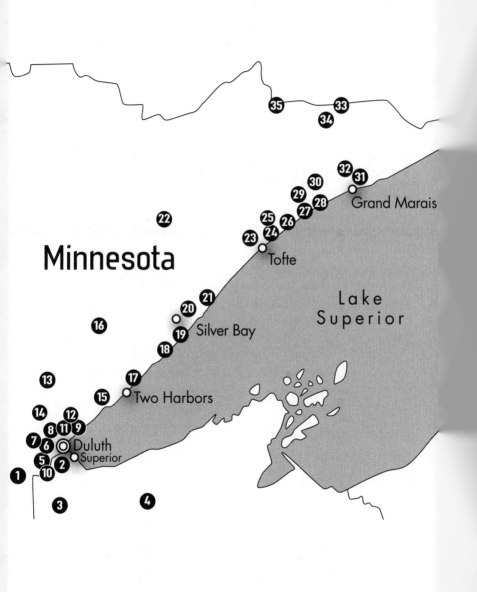

Why is North Shore skiing so darn good? Why do intelligent people give up on career advancement just to live near these trails? Why do families drive five hours each way for a few glorious hours in these woods?

There's no single answer to these questions. It's the rugged scenery and remote terrain. It's the winter weather, bringing more reliable snowfall to the North Shore than anywhere else in the state. It's the traditional hospitality passed down from generations.

A massive geologic event over one billion years ago created the foundation of the North Shore's current landscape. Layer after layer of lava and magma erupted from a huge rift in the earth's crust. These layers stacked up 20,000 feet high, then tilted in toward the center of what is now Lake Superior.

Glaciers from the last Ice Age scoured these layers down, leaving distinct ridges and valleys known now as the Sawtooth Mountains. The glaciers left behind the basin for the world's largest expanse of fresh water, Lake Superior.

The broad inland sea that settled next to these rugged ridges created the perfect combination of dramatic views and lake-effect climate. Now, the ridges of the North Shore have by far the highest annual snowfall and longest-lasting snow cover in Minnesota.

There's another reason why cross country skiing fits this region like a mitten on a ski pole—the people of the North Shore. The history of cross country skiing is long and mostly Scandinavian. It's no wonder that Minnesota, with its strong Scandinavian heritage, became such a hot spot for "Nordic" skiing.

But where the Swedes and Norwegians settled in the south and west of the state, it was the Finns who came to the North Shore and left their mark. Korkki Nordic in rural Duluth was an early center of skiing, with trails built by Charlie Banks in 1954 on land homesteaded by his Finnish father-in-law. A 1977 effort by Governor Rudy Perpich (a native of northeastern Minnesota) to make Minnesota the "Ski Touring Capital of the Nation" resulted in a flurry of activity with new standards, legislation and trail signage.

North Shore community members were responsible for most of the trails we see today. Local skiers and resort owners, with training from state and national clubs, made up crews that built hundreds, even thousands, of miles of ski trails. Trails such as those at Sugarbush were built with collaboration from resort owners, the Forest Service, and local residents. In Duluth, local volunteers joined with the city parks department to lace trails through the city's green spaces. One Finn built his own trails at Piedmont only to have them adopted by the city later on.

Why are these trails so darn good? Because time and nature and people have made it so.

Paying your dues

There is almost no such thing as a free ski outing. Despite the hard work of volunteers, some money is always necessary to fuel the chain saws and pay for the grooming equipment. If you find a trail that seems to be free, chances are there is an opportunity for you to help out either financially or physically. The North Shore is blessed with a tremendous wealth of skiing opportunities, thanks to skiers willing to pitch in and help out.

Minnesota state passes. The Great Minnesota Ski Pass is an incredible bargain. Passes are required at 20 of the 35 Minnesota areas described in this book. The pass generates funds through the DNR's Grant-In-Aid program for building, maintaining and grooming Minnesota ski trails. Passes are available on a daily basis, a yearly basis, or for three years. Passes can be purchased by phone, online or at state parks and many businesses.

Private areas. There are a number of cross country ski areas in the region that are privately owned and maintained. These areas charge their own usage fees, typically $5 to $12 a day. Often these trail fees are included in the cost of lodging for guests at the nearby resorts. Annual and family passes are often available. The Great Minnesota Ski Pass is generally not required at these private areas, but inquire locally to be sure.

For the extra cost, skiers will find consistently well-groomed trails, generally excellent facilities and a nice variety of skiing challenges. For the total skiing vacation, these facilities are an excellent choice.

Local clubs. The tradition of volunteering and local involvement has not been lost in the growth of private resorts and the statewide pass. In fact, anywhere you ski there is likely a local group working hard year-round to keep your skiing experience excellent. These groups survive on tiny annual budgets supported mostly by membership contributions. Addresses of local clubs are included in the "Resources" section (p. 150) of this book.

Since the statewide pass is such a good deal, take the time and the extra ten bucks or so to join and support one of these local clubs as well. Your money will be well spent. A little sweat equity always helps as well; you can donate time in the fall to clear trails, in the winter to fill bare spots, and in the spring to clear debris.

THE GREAT MINNESOTA SKI PASS

To ski on many public trails, you'll need a Great Minnesota Ski Pass sold by the Department of Natural Resources (DNR). Skiers age 16 and older must have a signed current ski pass in their possession when skiing on these designated trails.

A one-day pass is $5; a one-season pass is $15; and a three-season pass is $40. The Great Minnesota Ski Pass can be purchased a number of ways:

• ONLINE. Visit the DNR web site at www.dnr.state.mn.us/licenses/skipass/

• IN PERSON. All Minnesota state parks on the North Shore sell the ski pass, sometimes with a self-service box. You can also visit any Electronic License System vendor, like convenience stores, hardware stores and bait shops. Check the DNR's web site for a location near you.

• BY PHONE. You can purchase a pass 24 hours/day by calling 1-888-665-4236. A $3.50 fee is added for phone processing.

The pass really is required. If you are caught without a pass, the penalty is substantial. Bring the pass with you when you ski; if you accidentally leave it at home or in the car there could still be a penalty. ❄

Rules of the road

Regardless of where you ski, some basic rules of courtesy and safety apply.

Follow designated trail directions. This is for your safety and your enjoyment. One-way trails keep skiers from running into each other on hills and blind turns. They also keep skiing parties separate from each other, giving more of a wilderness feel to the experience.

Follow designated trail uses. Many trails are for both skate skiers and classical skiers. Skate skiers should keep their ski tips away from the classical track. Alternately, classical skiers should stay in the tracks and allow skate skiers to pass.

Dogs are not allowed on trails. With a few exceptions, dogs should not be taken on your ski outing. They scare away wildlife and mess up the groomed trail with their feet and their feces. With the growing popularity of skijoring, some ski areas have designated one of their trails for canine use. Other areas designate a day or two each week to bring your dog on the trail.

Fill in "sitzmarks" if you fall. That crater of snow left from your spill will easily lead to another fall for the next skier. Pack in the snow again, run your skis through the groomed track and make it safe again.

Ski under control. If that hill seems too steep for you, snowplow or sidestep down. It is even okay to take off your skis and walk. This is both for your safety and the safety of the people below.

Do not obstruct the trail. When you take a break, step out of the track so that others can ski by. This is especially important if you are on a hill.

When removing skis and walking, walk on the side of the trail. Try to keep the groomed trail as neat as possible for the next skiers. In general, ski trails should not be used for either snowshoeing or hiking in winter.

A word on trail ratings

The difficulty ratings used in this book for trail descriptions and in trail maps are taken from the original, locally produced trail maps. There is no standard rating system for ski areas, neither in the names of the levels nor in what they mean. In general, however, use the guidelines below. Where the ratings seem truly inaccurate, the text makes that point.

Some trails are labeled "Easy," "Easier," "Beginner" or marked with a circle. These are suitable for all skiers. The terrain is level; if there are uphills, skiers won't have to "herringbone" for more than a few feet, and any downhill will be easy with a long run-out and no turns.

Some trails are labeled "More Difficult," "Intermediate" or marked with a square. These trails have some hills. Short uphills require a herringbone climb, and downhills require some ability to turn.

Some trails are labeled "Advanced," "Expert," "Most Difficult" or marked with a diamond. These require advanced skills such as snowplow turns and extended herringbone climbing. Expect sharp and steep turns on downhills (including hairpin turns) and long climbs.

Andrew's Lists

The following lists are the author's somewhat arbitrary picks for top ski trails on the North Shore...all depending on what you are looking for. If your favorite isn't here, rest easy because absolutely no scientific procedure was applied.

Best grooming. Here are your best chances for smooth, fresh and neat grooming regardless of the conditions. Committed groomers come out first chance they get.

- Spirit Mountain
- Snowflake Nordic Center
- Boulder Lake
- Korkki Nordic Ski Center
- Gooseberry Falls State Park
- Sugarbush Trail System
- Solbakken Resort
- Cascade Lodge
- Pincushion Mountain
- Central Gunflint
- Upper Gunflint

Trails my mother would like. These have gentle loops, aren't crowded, but have a few easy hills and nice scenery.

- Jay Cooke State Park: CCC Trail
- Superior Municipal Forest: Red Loop
- Canosia Wildlife Management Area Trail
- Boulder Lake: Otter Run, Blue Ox
- Northwoods Ski Touring Trail: Inner Loops
- Flathorn-Gegoka: Central Loops
- Sugarbush Trail System: Wood Duck, Piece of Cake
- Cascade River State Park: Cedar Woods
- George Washington Trail
- Central Gunflint: Summer Home Road, Ox Cart Trail

Absolutely "free." These trails have no permits required or membership suggested.

- Canosia Wildlife Management Area Trail
- Boulder Lake
- George Washington Trail
- Bagley Nature Area

Most off the beaten path. On these trails you can really get away from it all.

- Jay Cooke State Park: Spruce, High trails
- Magney Ski Area
- Northwoods Ski Touring Trail: Tettegouche Connector
- Tettegouche State Park
- Sugarbush Trail System: Picnic Loop, Sixmile Crossing
- Banadad Trail
- Upper Gunflint: Magnetic Rock

Longest season. Deep snow away from Lake Superior's warmth, plus quality grooming, let you ski early and late.

- Afterhours Ski Trail
- Piedmont and Hartley Field trails
- Snowflake Nordic Center
- Flathorn-Gegoka
- Sugarbush Trail System: Moose Fence trailhead
- Sugarbush Trail System: Onion River Road trailhead
- Bally Creek
- Pincushion Mountain
- Gunflint Trail

Best views of Lake Superior. You might have to work for it, but you'll find great views from high bluffs or the shoreline.
- Piedmont Ski Trail
- Chester Park
- Gooseberry Falls State Park
- Split Rock Lighthouse State Park
- Cascade River State Park: Lakeshore Loop, Moose Mountain
- Pincushion Mountain

Best downhill routes. Arrange a car shuttle so you can do these "norpine" trails from ridgeline to lakeshore.
- Sawbill Trail to Tofte on Bluefin Trail
- Caribou Trail to Solbakken Resort
- Deer Yard to Cascade Lodge
- Bally Creek to Cascade River State Park

Best winter camping. Bring your winter camping gear and head out to these trails with remote campsites.
- Jay Cooke State Park
- Pattison State Park
- Boulder Lake (on ungroomed Wolf Bay Trail)
- Banadad Trail

Most family friendly. Out for the day? The following offer trails for beginner and advanced skiers, plus warming huts and restrooms.
- Afterhours Ski Trail
- Jay Cooke State Park
- Superior Municipal Forest
- Spirit Mountain
- Snowflake Nordic Center
- Korkki Nordic Ski Center
- Gooseberry Falls State Park
- Split Rock Lighthouse State Park
- Pincushion Mountain

Screamers. These downhill shots take your breath away. When you can't see the bottom from the top, get ready!
- Spirit Mountain: George Hovland 11K
- Piedmont Ski Trail: Expert Loop
- Lester-Amity: Upper Loop side hills

- Korkki Nordic Ski Center: Iso Maki Big Hill
- Gooseberry Falls State Park: Birch Hill loop
- Tettegouche State Park: Lower Loop
- Sugarbush Trail System: Bridge Run
- Central Gunflint: North-South Link, Overlook
- Upper Gunflint: West End Trail

FUN WITH SKI WAX

Avid skiers talk ski wax like baseball fans discuss hitting statistics. Here's a sample: "Well, it's in the 30s and I thought it was a klister day but I gobbed some yellow in the kick zone and I got some good grab." For equally incomprehensible fun, try reading aloud the Norwegian and Finnish instructions on the stubs of your leftover wax. Good waxing is a wonderful addition to your ski day, and bad waxing can be a serious detriment. Here are some tips:

- When in doubt, err on the "cold" side, especially in fresh snow. It's better to not stick than to stick too much.

- If you are slipping too much, the answer might be in your hands: try putting more weight on your poles.

- If that doesn't work, just apply some "TLC." "T" is for "thicker," i.e. apply your existing wax thicker. If that doesn't work, try "L" for "longer," filling in more of your kick zone with wax. Finally, you can try "C" for "change"—change to the next warmer wax. ❄

Duluth-Superior Area

This must be paradise. From anywhere within the city limits of Duluth and Superior, you are never more than a few miles away from terrific skiing. From the wild curves and vast views of little Chester Bowl to the backcountry pines of Boulder Lake, from winter camping at Pattison State Park to the races at Snowflake, the range of options will keep any skier busy winter-long. Plus, from Duluth you can hit either the South or North Shore, depending on where the snow is. Some of these trails roll through ball fields and backyards, others take you into wolf country. Whether you're visiting or living here, prepare for terrific skiing.

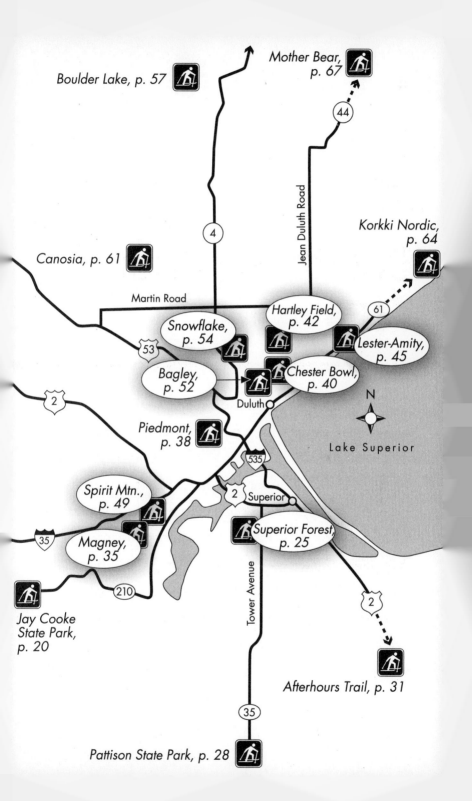

Boulder Lake, p. 57

Mother Bear, p. 67

44

Jean Duluth Road

Korkki Nordic, p. 64

Canosia, p. 61

4

Martin Road

61

Hartley Field, p. 42

Snowflake, p. 54

Lester-Amity, p. 45

53

Bagley, p. 52

Chester Bowl, p. 40

2

Duluth

N

Piedmont, p. 38

Lake Superior

535

Spirit Mtn., p. 49

2   Superior

35

Superior Forest, p. 25

Magney, p. 35

210

2

Jay Cooke State Park, p. 20

Tower Avenue

Afterhours Trail, p. 31

35

Pattison State Park, p. 28

Jay Cooke State Park

Carlton, Minnesota

Trailhead access
Drive three miles east of Carlton and Thomson on Highway 210 to the "Swinging Bridge" and the River Inn Visitor Center. Or drive from West Duluth and Fond du Lac west on Highway 210.

Total groomed trail: 48.1K
Classical skiing: 48.1K

Trail difficulty
Easy to advanced. Beginning skiers should stay on the north side of the swinging bridge, while advanced skiers have a wide range of terrain. If you're planning on skiing Spruce Trail, the trail on the edge of the system, call the park office ahead of time to see if it's been groomed.

Pass requirements
• Great Minnesota Ski Pass
• Minnesota State Park vehicle permit

Trailhead facilities
State park visitor center with restrooms, vending machines, fireplace. Both ski passes and vehicle permits are sold in the park office.

What makes it unique
There is an amazing amount of good skiing here within easy access of Duluth. You can walk across a dramatic swinging bridge over the St. Louis River—crossing a rushing river and sharp 1.6 billion-year-old metamorphic rocks—to reach ski trails on the south side of the park.

Information
Jay Cooke State Park, 500 E. Highway 210, Carlton MN 55718, (218) 384-4610. www.dnr.state.mn.us/state_parks/jay_cooke/

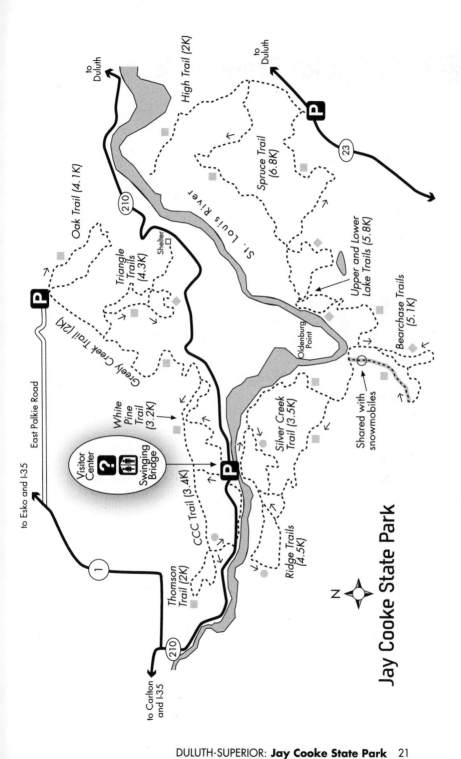

Jay Cooke State Park

South of Swinging Bridge

The toughest part about skiing these trails is getting across the bridge and up the first hill. Most people walk across the bridge and up the first hill. A little extra work to reach these trails gives you solitude and adventure.

RIDGE TRAILS (4.5K)

Easier. As the name implies, the Ridge Trails traverse a ridge above the St. Louis River; the ridge is thick with maples. With three smaller loops, this section is perfect for goofing around with young kids, if they can get there.

SILVER CREEK AND BEAR CHASE TRAILS (8.6K)

Intermediate and advanced. These trails begin to take you into the back country of the park. From here on, the farther you go, the fewer people you will see. From the bridge, the Silver Creek Trail is a 5K loop along the edge of the river valley with great views, returning along Silver Creek's wetlands back to the Ridge Trails. As long as you've come this far, cross Silver Creek and take the Bear Chase Trails too; the trails take you up tight valleys then down narrow ridges for a fun, advanced ride.

UPPER AND LOWER LAKE TRAILS (5.8K)

Advanced. These advanced trails will keep you huffing and puffing as you climb from the banks of the St. Louis River 200 feet up and glide back down again. These and the following trails are not groomed as often as the inner trails, so you should check with the park ranger before heading out here for the day. Watch out on steep two-way trails.

SPRUCE AND HIGH TRAILS (8.8K)

Intermediate. Once past the advanced Lost Lake trails you enter more level, intermediate country which you're almost guaranteed to have all to yourself. The Spruce Trail itself is a 6.8K loop through cedar, pines and maple, with the southern half having constant views off the bluff; if that's not enough, take the High Trail 2K to an overlook of the St. Louis River. You can also access these trails from a small parking area on Highway 23.

North of Swinging Bridge

The trails north of the bridge start from the parking lot on the opposite side of the park office. Most skiers walk the thirty yards to Highway 210 and cross it before putting on their skis.

CCC TRAIL (3.4K)

Easier. This trail takes old roadways through relatively open terrain around the campground. The eastern half in particular is very easy going after the first climb. The western half gets trickier when the trail leaves the old roadway and winds down to cross Highway 210. The return along the river bank is scenic any time of year.

WHITE PINE TRAIL (3.2K)

Intermediate. This is a delightful loop through dense groves of white pine and an open maple ridgeline. The first 0.4K follows an old roadbed downhill; the trail turns left off the old road and starts climbing for a long herringbone up and around to a shelter with a great view of the St. Louis River valley. Enjoy a snack here as you take off for a day's ski. The trail winds through some rolling terrain on the south side, then levels out on the north side. Some of the turns are tricky here, so be prepared for quick moves.

THOMSON TRAIL (2K)

Intermediate. This is made "intermediate" by a daring swoop down and up past some large white pine. Otherwise this is mostly level terrain through open deciduous woods.

GREELY CREEK TRAIL (2K)

Intermediate. This trail connects the Oldenburg Point trails and the White Pine trails with the Triangle and Oak loops. The trail gives you a close-up look at the Thomson hydropower operations of Minnesota Power as it follows power lines and then skirts the shore of Forbay Lake before crossing over the top of the small dam.

TRIANGLE TRAILS (4.3K)

Intermediate to advanced. Noticeably more difficult than the Oak Trails, this 2.2K loop rolls through a variety of forests, with a spur to a shelter. The 1.3K advanced side trail, which dips off the plateau and into the hillside, is pretty wild and may not be groomed.

OAK TRAIL (4.1K)

Intermediate. Access this loop from the Greely Creek Trail or more commonly from Palkie Road, 1.6 miles east of County Road 1. This trail is remarkably level as it curves around the rim of a plateau. As the name implies, there are lots of oak here, plus some great views to distant ridges.

SHIVER LIKE A CHICKADEE

The black-capped chickadee has a "bundle" of survival tricks, including bundling. On cold nights, chickadees will gather in a flock of about six birds and bundle together in the hole of an evergreen tree, keeping each other warm through the night. The chickadees will go into a sort of torpor, letting their body temperatures drop as much as 12° C. They maintain this temperature all night, through outbreaks of group shivering.

Next time you're out with a group and it's getting cold, get a group hug going and have everybody shimmy to stay toasty! ❄

Superior Municipal Forest

Superior, Wisconsin

Trailhead access

There are two trailheads: **(1)** Take 28th Street one mile west from Tower Avenue. Parking lot is on south side of road, marked with a sign; or **(2)** Continue on 28th Street until it turns into Billings Drive. Follow Billings Drive for about two miles to the parking lot on the left with the ski trail signage.

Total groomed trail: 26K

Classical skiing: 26K   Skate skiing: 26K

Trail difficulty

Beginners should stick to the 28th Street trailhead, with the easier trails. Advanced skiers will enjoy the Billings Drive trailhead, with quick access to the physically challenging Yellow Loop.

Pass requirements

• Day passes ($5) and season passes ($20–$30) available at trailheads. Passes required for ages 16 and older; senior discount available.

Trailhead facilities

Restrooms and warming hut at 28th Street trailhead.

Snow conditions: (715) 395-7299

What makes it unique

A wide variety of terrain is found in the country's second largest municipal forest. The system is ranked as one of Wisconsin's best cross country ski trails. The trails are groomed quite wide, so both skate skiers and classical skiers have plenty of room.

Information

Superior Parks and Recreation Department, 1407 Hammond Avenue, Superior WI 54880, (715) 394-0270.
www.ci.superior.wi.us

RED TRAILS—INNER AND OUTER (3K)

Easy. This is a wide, level warm-up trail, great for families and first-time skiers. Towering pines give this loop a cozy feel. Both the inner and outer trail lead from one "island" of white pines to another; these "islands" are on ground that is just a few feet higher than the "sea" of alder, which are on lower, wetter ground.

BLUE TRAIL (2K)

Advanced. There are so many fun ups and downs on this trail it feels much longer than 2K. Nice boreal forest and wild hills distinguish this short section from the rest of the trails in the Superior Municipal Forest.

GREEN TRAILS (INNER AND OUTER) (5K)

Intermediate. This network of trails runs through fields and open woods, zooming down to cross the occasional stream and then up the other side. Although all trails are two-way, most people take these trails counterclockwise (as indicated by the arrows posted on the trails). The trails on the north and west sides take you into more ambitious terrain, with hills and turns, but for the most part this is family-friendly and fun.

YELLOW LOOP (10K)

Advanced. Access this trail from the Billings Drive trailhead. There are some serious downhills followed by grunting uphills on the eastern side of the loop, as the trail descends into valleys of the streams that empty into the St. Louis River estuary. Almost all of these downward swoops can be bypassed with side loops. Take the Cedar Point spur trail and you can get out onto Kimball's Bay for some skate skiing if the conditions are right. Settle into a zen-like groove on the return side of the loop, as the terrain and forest hardly changes for over 2K.

PURPLE TRAIL (6K)

Advanced. Two-thirds of the Purple Trail is alongside a snow-mobile trail, so be prepared to share this loop with snowmobiles.

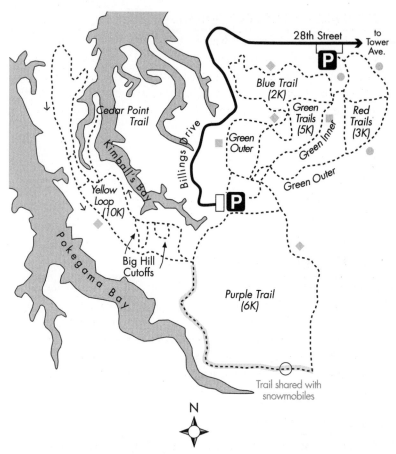

Superior Municipal Forest

In the shared section, the classical trail is either not set or gets quickly erased by snowmobiles. You'll get right to the edge of Kimball's and Pokegama Bay on this trail…it's hard to imagine these shallow, quiet bays are actually considered to be part of Lake Superior. As the eastern third is the only part not shared with snowmobiles, this trail is best suited for skate skiing.

Note: Skijorers can use the multiple-use Orange Trail off of Central Avenue on Chase's Point.

Pattison State Park

Superior, Wisconsin

Trailhead access
Drive 12 miles south of Superior on Highway 35 (not Interstate 35). Take park road toward campground and continue driving to ski trailhead.

Total groomed trail: 7K
Classical skiing: 7K

Trail difficulty
Like a lot of trail systems, the further out you get, the more challenging the trails are. All but beginner skiers can easily do all the trails here in an hour or two.

Pass requirements
• Wisconsin state park vehicle permit. One hour permits ($3), day permits ($7 Wisconsin residents, $10 non-Wisconsin residents) and season permits ($25 Wisconsin residents, $35 non-Wisconsin residents); all available at park office.

Trailhead facilities
Restroom at park office.

What makes it unique
This trail system gives you a flavor of a different sort of forest than the North Shore. Large basswoods and oaks mix in with the stands of maple. In the winter it's hard to tell these trees apart, but with some practice, you can do it on the fly. For an extra adventure, ski in to the campsites on the Orange Loop for a night of winter camping. Check at the park office for details.

Information
Park Superintendent, 6294 S. State Road 35, Superior WI 54880, (715) 399-3111. www.dnr.state.wi.us

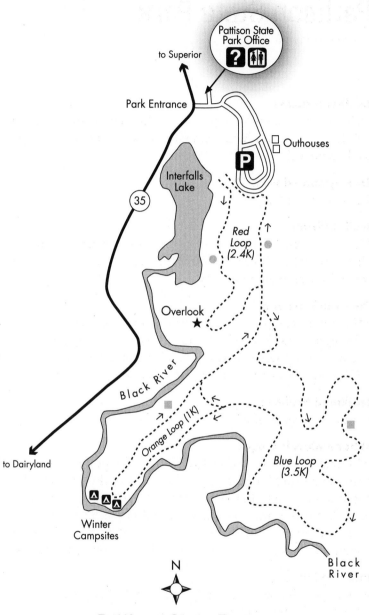

Pattison State Park
Park Office
? 🚻

to Superior

Park Entrance

🅿

Outhouses

Interfalls
Lake

35

*Red
Loop
(2.4K)*

Overlook
★

Black River

to Dairyland

Orange Loop (1K)

*Blue Loop
(3.5K)*

Winter
Campsites

Black
River

N

Pattison State Park

RED LOOP (2.4K)

Easier. This mostly level loop starts off near an historic forestry facility, passes some maintenance buildings, then enters a nice maple and oak forest. At the halfway point, there is an overlook of the Black River valley.

BLUE LOOP (3.5K)

Intermediate. This winding, relatively easy loop takes you clockwise through a quiet and remote corner of the park. The last half of the loop runs along the Black River, with nice views of the river. Watch for extra large yellow birch and white pine trees along the trail. Trail runs past an 1880s logging camp.

ORANGE LOOP (1K)

Intermediate. This short loop has plenty of turns and short hills through pockets of birch and fir. A shelter at the far end of the loop marks the entrance to three backpack campsites on the Black River just above Little Manitou Falls (there are outhouses available by the campsites). These are used infrequently in winter.

POPPING BIRCHES

It's a cold you can feel deep in your body, your breath sending icy knives into the recesses of your lungs. Luckily, it's just a short walk up the driveway before turning in. A dangerous cold, with the night sky so starry you know it will get even colder. Tonight will be a far cry from the warmth of the afternoon, when winter sun warmed the hillsides and the birch trees, melting the sap within. Now, with the return of the real cold, the sap freezes again—and freezes fast. The freezing sap expands and cracks open the side of the birch with a muffled gunshot. You think "what's that?" and then you remember: it's February, the Moon of the Popping Trees. ❄

Afterhours Ski Trail

Brule, Wisconsin

Trailhead access
On U.S. Highway 2, 30 miles east of Superior, Wisconsin at the edge of the South Shore snow belt. Just west of downtown Brule, turn south on Afterhours Road directly into the parking lot.

Total groomed trail: 23.4K
Classical skiing: 23.4K   Skate skiing: 20.8K

Trail difficulty
Mostly intermediate terrain here. Trails are groomed quite wide, so only the steepest hills and turns down by the river present a real challenge.

Pass Requirements
• Annual ($15) and daily ($4) passes sold at the trailhead. Under 16 ski free. The Brule Valley Ski Club works with Brule River State Forest to maintain and improve the trail system. The club welcomes annual memberships; look for details at the trailhead.

Trailhead Facilities
Warming hut, outhouse. The town of Brule has restaurants, gas stations, and a motel.

What makes it unique
If you want to ski the North Shore but all the snow has fallen on the South Shore, this is your easiest opportunity to enjoy lake-effect snowbelt skiing. Duluth can be totally brown, but as you drive east past Poplar and Maple, suddenly the snow piles up. Here, early season skiing can start in mid-November.

Information
Park Superintendent, Brule River State Forest,
6250 S. Ranger Road, Brule WI 54820, 715-372-5678.
www.brulexcski.com   www.norwiski.com

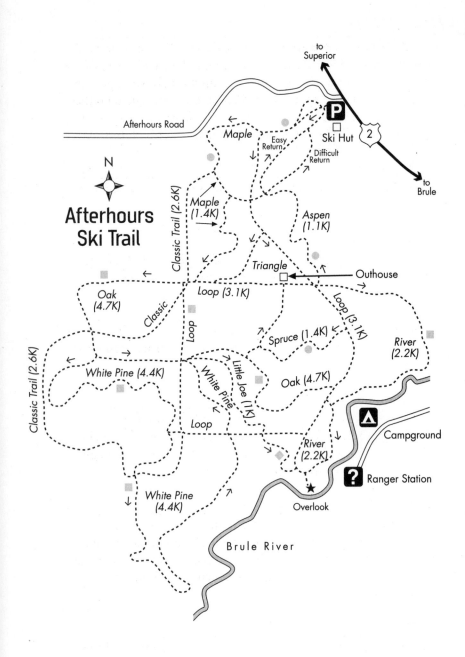

Afterhours Ski Trail

N

Afterhours Road

Maple

Easy Return

Difficult Return

to Superior

Ski Hut

2

to Brule

Classic Trail (2.6K)

Maple (1.4K)

Aspen (1.1K)

Triangle

Outhouse

Loop (3.1K)

Oak (4.7K)

Classic

Loop

Loop (3.1K)

White Pine

Little Joe (1K)

Spruce (1.4K)

River (2.2K)

Classic Trail (2.6K)

White Pine (4.4K)

Oak (4.7K)

Loop

River (2.2K)

Campground

Ranger Station

White Pine (4.4K)

Overlook

Brule River

ENTRY (1.5K)

Beginner and advanced. Choices, choices. Easy start or hard? Easy return or difficult? Everyone starting these trails makes these choices right away, but both trails roll up through white pine to the same spot, Hilltop Junction, then onto the triangle trails that connect to the Loop trail. On the way back, it's the classic end-of-ski downhill run, either easy or difficult—but both fun.

MAPLE (1.4K)

Beginner. Gentle curves take you through sugar maple forest.

CLASSIC (2.6K)

Intermediate. Weaving through the western half of the system, this narrow trail gives classical skiers their own delightful loop. In some conditions, this is the best skiing in the system.

ASPEN (1.1K)

Beginner. This is the main one-way trail taking you back to the trailhead. It's curvy but easy. Take it after the Spruce Trail for a beginner route.

SPRUCE (1.4K)

Beginner. Nice flat trail that is lined with the distinctive Norway spruce, an exotic tree noted for its drooping branches. This connects with the Entry and Aspen trails for a fun beginner route of about 4K.

OAK (4.7K)

Intermediate. Starts easy and flat, following an unplowed, summer-only road straight to the west. Things get interesting when you finally turn left, crossing wetland areas, passing large Norway spruce, and winding back down toward the Brule River valley.

RIVER (2.2K)

Intermediate. When the snow is fresh, this is considered the best trail in the system, with great downhill runs, views of the

Brule River, even wolf scat. The pine forest can leave needles on the trail. This is the route of an 1890s logging railroad and was the route used by early Brule River vacationers to reach their camps. A spur trail leads to Little Joe Lookout, with a view of Little Joe Rapids, before bending back to the north.

WHITE PINE (4.4K)

Intermediate. This is a long winding trail that starts in lots of white pine and then descends toward the river valley into open aspen woods. Take a break at the old, gnarled jack pine overlooking the Brule River valley before starting the gentle climb back up.

LOOP (3.1K)

Intermediate. This is signed as "North Loop," "West Loop," "South Loop" and "East Loop," but it's all one trail, mostly flat, easy and wide. Near the "Northeast Junction" is an unmarked outhouse.

LITTLE JOE (1.0K)

Advanced. This is rated advanced because of the wild roller coaster near its end at the River Trail by the Little Joe Rapids lookout. It feels like running a slalom course, with large white pines as the slalom gates.

GREAT SNACKS FOR YOUR FANNY PACK

What's compact, hard to break, won't freeze, and is full of complex carbohydrates? The ideal trail snack, that's what! For outings longer than an hour, pack away some extra fuel like raisins, peanuts or their yogurt-covered cousins. Hard cheeses hold up well, but slice them before you head out. For a trail lunch, nothing's more delicious than a bagel with meat or cheese. Don't bother with anything wrapped up like chocolate candies; you'll be a litterbug for sure. Also, keep a water bottle inside your pack to prevent it from freezing. ❋

Magney Ski Area
Duluth, Minnesota

Trailhead access
Take Interstate 35 to Boundary Avenue exit. Drive 2.5 miles on Skyline Parkway (past Spirit Mountain recreation area), following the road signs for "Magney Ski Area." Parking lot is on left side at end of plowed road; trailhead is on right side of road.

Total groomed trail: 13K
Classical skiing: 13K   Skate skiing: 13K

Trail difficulty
Magney Ski Area has long, challenging loops, difficult both for the hills and turns but also for their length. Although groomed and designated for skating, the trail is narrow and tracked at the edge, so classical skiers should watch out for overhanging branches.

Pass requirements
• Great Minnesota Ski Pass

Trailhead facilities
None

Snow conditions: (218) 730-4321

What makes it unique
The extensive old-growth maple forest and remote-feeling terrain give this in-town ski area a terrific wilderness feel. Judge Clarence R. Magney was a critical early advocate for both city and state parks along the North Shore.

Information
Parks and Recreation Dept., 12 East Fourth Street, Duluth MN 55805, (218) 730-4300.
www.ci.duluth.mn.us/city/parksandrecreation

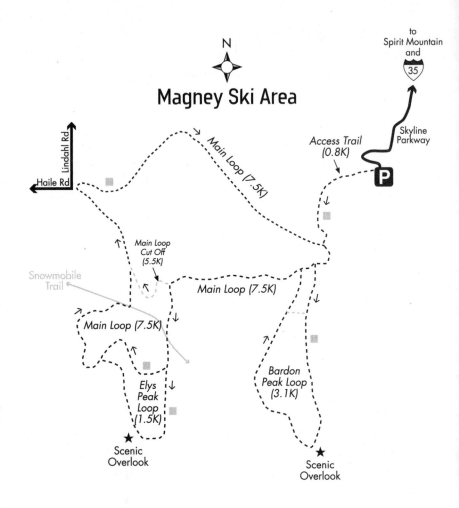

Magney Ski Area

N

to Spirit Mountain and 35

Lindahl Rd

Haile Rd

Main Loop (7.5K)

Access Trail (0.8K)

Skyline Parkway

P

Main Loop Cut Off (5.5K)

Snowmobile Trail

Main Loop (7.5K)

Main Loop (7.5K)

Elys Peak Loop (1.5K)

Bardon Peak Loop (3.1K)

★ Scenic Overlook

★ Scenic Overlook

FULL LOOP (7.5K)

Intermediate. After a 0.8K uphill ski on the access trail, you enter the most wild, natural and remote of Duluth's ski trails. The trail is marked by long, sometimes steep climbs and smooth, glorious downhills. There's a cutoff right after crossing the snowmobile trail that allows you to shorten the loop to 5.5K.

Although this is designated as a skating trail, it's fairly narrow, especially as winter snows weigh down trailside branches.

ELYS PEAK LOOP (1.5K)

Intermediate. Add this short section to get to a scenic overlook of the beautiful view of the valley below, including Elys Peak a half mile south.

BARDON PEAK LOOP (3.1K)

Intermediate and advanced. Soon after joining the main loop from the 0.8K access trail, you will reach the Bardon Peak Loop juncture. This loop and its tremendous overlook offers a view of Duluth, Superior and the St. Louis River valley below. Climb up into maple woods and descend into ash swamps before rejoining the main trail. If you liked it the first time, do it again! A cut-off 0.5K in allows you to avoid the advanced section.

DULUTH'S FABULOUS CITY PARKS:
Magney Ski Area, Piedmont Ski Trail, Chester Bowl, Hartley Field, and Lester-Amity Ski Areas

Scattered across the rugged hills of Duluth are some of the finest urban ski trails anywhere, period. Five different city parks with 47K of groomed trails await your sampling, ranging from the short but sweet racer's loop at Chester Bowl to the diverse network of trails at Lester-Amity; from the back country of Magney Ski Area to the your-own-backyard atmosphere of Piedmont Ski Trail.

Grooming is regular and professional. For the latest grooming update, call the hotline at 730-4321 before heading out to ski. The trailheads have few facilities, but are all within a mile of whatever you might need. ❅

Piedmont Ski Trail

Duluth, Minnesota

Trailhead access
From the stoplight on U.S. 53, take Piedmont Avenue two
blocks and turn left on Hutchinson Road. Take Hutchinson
Road 0.7 miles uphill to parking lot on the left side of road,
near the corner of Adirondack Street.

Total groomed trail: 6K
Classical skiing: 6K

Trail difficulty
The main loop here attracts mostly families and friends, enjoying
the relatively easy double set of tracks with fun and conversation.
The Expert Loop and the trail beyond the "Chicken Loop Cut-
Off" are definitely for more advanced skiers.

Pass requirements
• Great Minnesota Ski Pass

Trailhead facilities
None

Snow conditions: (218) 730-4321

What makes it unique
This trail has homespun flavor and character. It was built by
Piedmont resident Jerry Nowak, and then turned over to the
City of Duluth for management. The clever signs along the trail
keep you laughing, and the in-town ease of getting here makes
for a quick and satisfying lunchtime fitness break.

Information
Parks and Recreation Dept., 12 East Fourth Street,
Duluth MN 55805, (218) 730-4300.
www.ci.duluth.mn.us/city/parksandrecreation

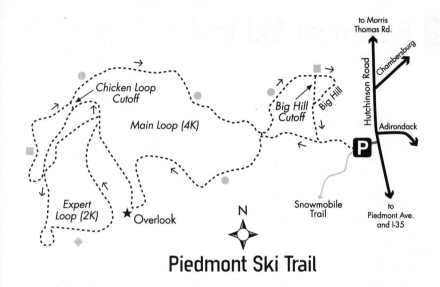

Piedmont Ski Trail

MAIN LOOP (4K)

Intermediate. Clever signs urge you on past small dips through a nicely mixed deciduous forest as you climb very gradually to a dramatic overlook, one of the best on Duluth trails. Double-tracked, the trail is generally well-suited for beginners, but watch out for the two exceptions. A short, fun advanced loop at the end can be bypassed by a 50-foot cutoff ("Chicken Loop"), and the big hill at the end can be bypassed by turning right at the "Piker's Peak" sign.

EXPERT LOOP (2K)

Advanced. This provides about 2K of steep hills and sharp turns on the edge of the bluff. Nice pine trees add to the thrill as you zoom down. Snow conditions on this loop can be marginal; a 50-meter shortcut at the start of the biggest hill lets you avoid the steepest down and up.

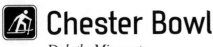

Chester Bowl

Duluth, Minnesota

Trailhead access
Take Skyline Parkway to the Chester Bowl Ski Area, either east from Kenwood Avenue or west from College Street and 19th Avenue East.

Total groomed trail: 3K
Classical skiing: 3K   Skate skiing: 3K

Trail difficulty
Best used only by advanced skiers. Screaming downhills with tight turns can have dogs, boot tracks or other obstacles, so it's good to have control.

Pass requirements
• Great Minnesota Ski Pass

Trailhead facilities
Chalet and restrooms open weekends and some evenings.

Snow conditions: (218) 730-4321

What makes it unique
This is a wild and woolly in-town ski area specifically for advanced skiers and racers. With downhill ski runs and a chair-lift in the park, Chester Bowl can be a complete ski outing.

Information
Parks and Recreation Dept., 12 East Fourth Street, Duluth MN 55805, (218) 730-4300.
www.ci.duluth.mn.us/city/parksandrecreation

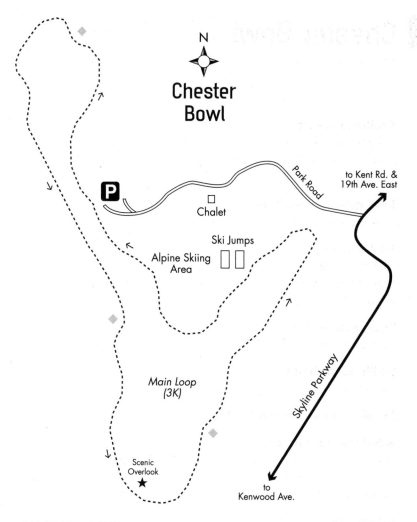

MAIN LOOP (3K)

Advanced. This is designed for advanced skiers, with serious downhills and turns. After a level start, you will cross Chester Creek and start on a roller coaster, up and down and around tight corners. About halfway is a field with a 120° view of Lake Superior. After the field, descend into the forest before one last climb up above the Chester Bowl chairlift for a final run back to where you began three hairy kilometers before. You may be sharing it with dog walkers, despite signs that prohibit dogs.

Hartley Field
Duluth, Minnesota

Trailhead access
There are three trailheads: **(1)** Use Hartley Nature Center parking lot, **(2)** Take Fairmont Road two blocks from Woodland Avenue, or **(3)** Take Hartley Road 0.3 miles from four-way stop at Arrowhead Road.

Total groomed trail: 5K
Classical skiing: 5K

Trail difficulty
This can be a great trail for a family outing, but parents should familiarize themselves with the trail beforehand. Steeper hills that will dump any five-year-old are scattered throughout the system.

Pass requirements
• Great Minnesota Ski Pass

Trailhead facilities
Restrooms at Nature Center.

Snow conditions: (218) 730-4321

What makes it unique
Nicely wooded double-tracked classic-only trails are a cozy alternative to other Duluth trails. The deep shady woods tend to hold on to late-season snow. On Saturdays, you can enjoy the warmth and restrooms of the Hartley Nature Center.

Information
Parks and Recreation Dept., 12 East Fourth Street, Duluth MN 55805, (218) 730-4300.
www.ci.duluth.mn.us/city/parksandrecreation

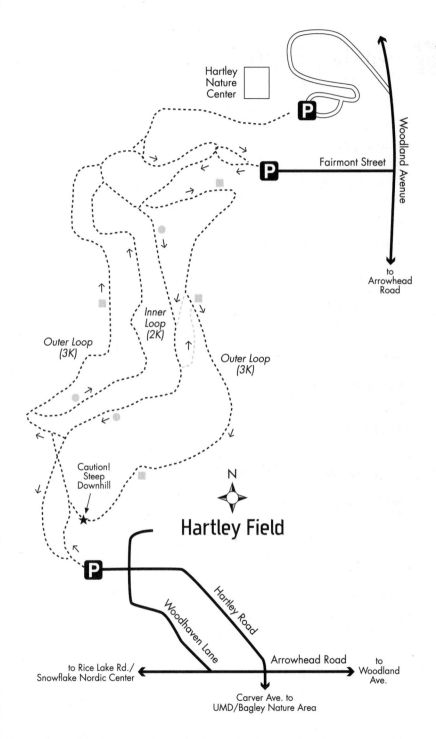

Hartley
Nature
Center

P

Woodland Avenue

P   Fairmont Street

to
Arrowhead
Road

Inner
Loop
(2K)

Outer Loop
(3K)

Outer Loop
(3K)

Caution!
Steep
Downhill

★

N

Hartley Field

P

Hartley Road

Woodhaven Lane

Arrowhead Road

to Rice Lake Rd./
Snowflake Nordic Center

to
Woodland
Ave.

Carver Ave. to
UMD/Bagley Nature Area

INNER LOOP (2K)

Easy. This loop is largely easygoing for the beginner, with just enough hills to provide for the beginner's "learning experiences" (also known as falls). The true beginning skier should start at the Nature Center trailhead to avoid a big downhill on the access trails. With few brief wrong-way turns, you can make a nice interconnected set of loops here.

OUTER LOOP (3K)

Intermediate. This is a wilder ride, especially on the eastern half, with hills both to climb and glide down. Turns come sharp and quick. There are nice views of Hartley's "Rock Knob" along the west side of the loop. The downhill at the southern end of the loop is particularly challenging.

A SKIER'S CALENDAR

NOVEMBER: Watch the forecast. You might get lucky late in the month, especially uphill and inland. Some people ski on golf courses.

DECEMBER: Grooming starts in earnest as snow fills in all the trails.

JANUARY: It's cold but snowy. Martin Luther King holiday weekend is busy with skiers on the North Shore.

FEBRUARY: This is peak skiing time, especially over the Presidents' Day weekend.

MARCH: Afternoons turn warm and start to melt the snow; bring no-wax skis if you have them. There's a mid- to late-morning magic hour when the temperature first rises above freezing, and before it turns too warm.

APRIL: Grooming's over, but there could still be snow in shady areas. The Onion River Road is often the last usable trail on the North Shore.

Lester-Amity

Duluth, Minnesota

Trailhead access
There are four trailheads: **(1)** Take Lester River Road 100
yards up from Superior Street to large parking lot on left;
(2) Take Seven Bridges Road (Occidental Boulevard) to road-
side parking about one mile from Superior Street; **(3)** On Seven
Bridges Road, drive farther uphill to Lakeside chalet parking
area on right; or **(4)** Take Lester River Road about 0.5 mile past
Trailhead 1 to the golf course on the right.

Total groomed trail: 16.8K
Classical skiing: 16.8K   Skate skiing: 16.8K   Lighted trail: 6K

Trail difficulty
There's a bit of everything here. Everyone starts with the easier
Inner Loops, but the upper loops provide real challenge,
especially with all the side loops.

Pass requirements
• Great Minnesota Ski Pass

Trailhead facilities
None

Snow conditions: (218) 730-4321

What makes it unique
Lots of skiing on the edge of the city makes for a popular trail;
the 6K of lighted trails are especially popular from dusk until
late evening. The dramatic and majestic white pines along
the lower loop by Amity Creek are a remnant of a forest that
covered much of this area.

Information
Parks and Recreation Dept., 12 East Fourth Street,
Duluth MN 55805, (218) 730-4300.
www.ci.duluth.mn.us/city/parksandrecreation

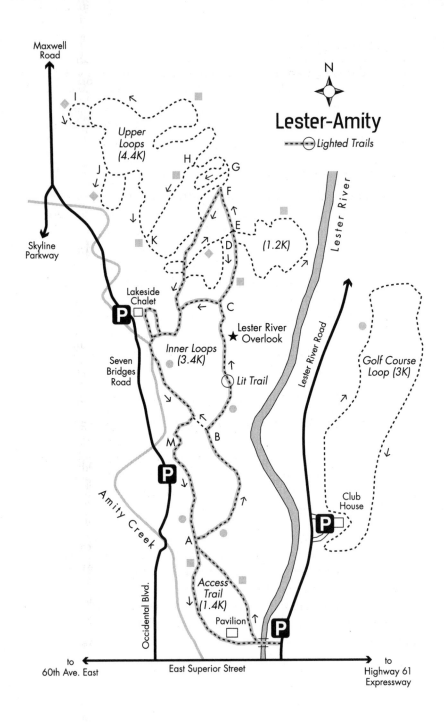

Maxwell Road

N

Lester-Amity

━━○ Lighted Trails

I

Upper Loops (4.4K)

J

H

G

F

K

E

D

C

(1.2K)

Lester River

Lakeside Chalet

Lester River Overlook

Seven Bridges Road

Inner Loops (3.4K)

○ Lit Trail

Lester River Road

Golf Course Loop (3K)

Skyline Parkway

M

B

A

Amity Creek

Occidental Blvd.

Club House

Access Trail (1.4K)

Pavilion

to 60th Ave. East

East Superior Street

to Highway 61 Expressway

ACCESS TRAIL (1.4K)

Intermediate/lighted. From the Lester River Road trailhead, cross the bridge, then climb through majestic white pine after crossing the open field. The first climb is pretty steep. On the downhill run back into the open park field you'll glide by huge pines and the scenic river—a real North Woods treat!

INNER LOOP (A-B-C) (3.4K)

Easy/lighted. This is a very popular 3.4K loop, which divides into a 1.7K southern loop that is a little hillier (one long, gradual climb and one long, gradual downhill) and a 1.7K northern loop that is a little flatter. Most people start this loop from the lower Seven Bridges Road parking lot. The wide trail leads through an open forest of birch and aspen. A few short dips keep you on your toes. The northern loop has a nice overlook of the Lester River. Expect to share the trail with speedy skate skiers and leisurely families. One side loop connects with the Lakeside Chalet; in early season conditions, when there's more snow away from the lake, you can park by the Chalet and just ski the northern loop.

UPPER LOOPS (C-D-F-G-H-J-K) (4.4K plus side loops)

Intermediate and advanced/C-D-F lighted. This is really two trails. The main trail is 4.4K of intermediate skiing through mixed forest. It's a gradual climb into level terrain, followed by a bit of a roller coaster ride down. You'll get away from the crowds on this loop. You can add a nice, relatively level 1.2K intermediate side loop on the way up.

The Upper Loops can also be an expert trail by adding the six advanced side loops, each about 0.5K. Each advanced side loop has both a steep climb and descent, not necessarily in that order. If you do all the side loops, this section ends up being around 9K. Caution: If you're not up for the hills and turns, watch out at intersections "I" and "J;" the intermediate trail goes left while the advanced trail goes straight ahead.

The Upper Loops tend to have better snow conditions than the lower loops.

GOLF COURSE LOOP (3K)

Easy/skijoring. The open, rolling terrain of the Lester Park Golf Course makes for a radically different skiing experience than the rest of Lester-Amity. This is not lighted, but is skiable at night by full moon (at your own risk). Grooming is a bit less frequent than the rest of the trails, but it's the only Duluth city park trail open to skijoring. Nice views of Lake Superior from the upper parts. Park at the golf course clubhouse, 0.4 miles up Lester River Road from Superior Street.

BE PREPARED ON LONGER JOURNEYS

Taking off on a long ski loop on the North Shore can bring you into remote and difficult terrain. You could be the only skier out that day. Cellphone coverage is spotty or nonexistent. Be prepared! In addition to supplies like ski wax and moleskin, you should consider bringing a small pack with the following:

- at least one quart of water per person

- high-energy snacks and/or bag lunch

- hat

- area map

- matches

- first aid kit

- extra insulation layer, like a compressible down jacket, for rest breaks

- flashlight

- ski repair kit: tape and replacement ski tip.

Remember that it's not enough just to bring the right stuff. You have to know when and how to use it. ❄

Spirit Mountain

Duluth, Minnesota

Trailhead access
Take Skyline Drive from Interstate 35 (Exit #249) and follow signs to Spirit Mountain Recreation Area. Stay on Skyline Drive past entrance to downhill ski area on left. Watch for turn on right side marked for the campground and Nordic center.

Total groomed trail: 22K
Classical skiing: 22K   Skate skiing: 22K   Lighted trail: 2K

Pass requirements
• Day passes ($7) and season passes ($80) for sale at trailhead chalet.

Trail difficulty
This system is best for intermediate and advanced skiers. Most of the trails, even the Eric Judeen beginner trail, are reached by an access trail that would be rated intermediate. Real beginners can use the Larry Sorenson 2K loop in the campground.

Trailhead facilities
Chalet, restrooms, snacks, equipment rentals.

Snow conditions: Call Nordic Center at (218) 624-8533

What makes it unique
This trail system is professionally groomed and it often provides the best and most consistent skiing conditions in Duluth. Early season skiers might find groomed trails on man-made snow. The presence of extensive old-growth forest helped to stop a proposed golf course development here.

Information
Spirit Mountain, 9500 Spirit Mountain Place, Duluth MN 55810, (218) 624-8533. www.spiritmt.com

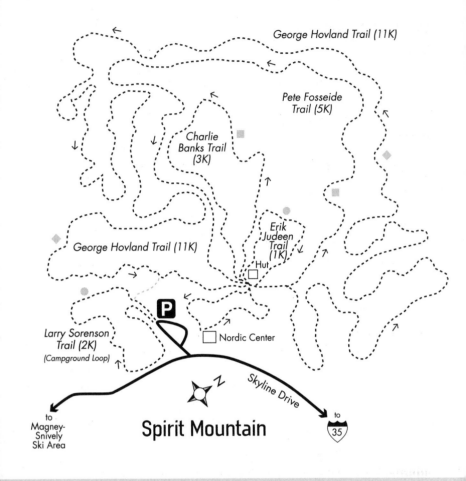

George Hovland Trail (11K)

Pete Fosseide
Trail (5K)

Charlie
Banks Trail
(3K)

George Hovland Trail (11K)

Erik
Judeen
Trail
(1K)

Hut

P

Nordic Center

Larry Sorenson
Trail (2K)
(Campground Loop)

Skyline Drive

N

Spirit Mountain

to
Magney-
Snively
Ski Area

to
35

LEGENDS OF SKIING

The trails at Spirit Mountain pay tribute to the legends of Northeastern Minnesota skiing. For example, Erik Judeen and Pete Fosseide were buddies who established Duluth's first ski trails in Chester Bowl. Pete won the 1938 three-day, 153-mile ski race from Duluth to St. Paul. Charlie Banks developed the trails now known as Korkki Nordic Ski Center in the 1950s. George Hovland, who developed both these trails and those at Snowflake Nordic Center, was on the 1952 Olympic ski team in Oslo. ❄

ERIK JUDEEN TRAIL (1K)

Beginner. Easy loop popular with families and used for ski lessons. Follow the green dots on a gradual climb to a sharp turn, then wind easily back to the warming hut.

CHARLIE BANKS TRAIL (3K)

Intermediate. This loop starts off tricky and then eases off. "Denis' Demise" is the biggest hill on the intermediate trails. Otherwise, this is a gently rolling trail, marked by yellow dots, that stays in old-growth forest on top of the plateau.

SPIRIT MOUNTAIN VILLAS

The octagonal villas are located trailside and slopeside. Four villas are adjacent to the Nordic trails. For information and reservations: (866) 688-4552 or www.mtvillas.com

PETE FOSSEIDE TRAIL (5K)

Intermediate. A little more challenging overall than the Charlie Banks Trail, this loop also brings you into a younger, more diverse forest. Following the blue dots, this trail takes you off of a plateau with a series of downhills just as you start. The terrain then levels out as you circle around the backside of the plateau and return to the warming hut.

GEORGE HOVLAND TRAIL (11K)

Intermediate to expert. This loop is for the ambitious, experienced skier. It's the longest uninterrupted loop in northeastern Minnesota and seems to get steeper and more curvy as it goes. If you get tired from the length or the hills, watch for intersections with the 5K loop where you can bail out. Save enough energy to whoop and holler at "Omagod" hill.

LARRY SORENSON TRAIL (CAMPGROUND LOOP) (2K)

Beginner/lighted. This easy loop through the summer campground is lighted for night skiing. The loop starts and ends with gradual downhills. The gentle climb between has nice views through the trees of the St. Louis River valley. Spirit Mountain is considering installing snowmaking equipment on this trail.

Bagley Nature Area
Duluth, Minnesota

Trailhead access
Take St. Marie Street from Woodland Avenue to the Bagley Nature Area parking lot near Oakland Apartments.

Total groomed trail: 2.7K
Classical skiing: 2.7K

Trail difficulty
Fairly challenging trails for general usage. Real beginners should stick to the short-cut version of the East Loop.

Pass requirements
• None. Parking meters at trailhead enforced 8am to 8pm, Monday through Friday; 25¢ for each 30 minutes.

Trailhead facilities
Outhouse

What makes it unique
A great asset for students is also available for community use. Bring a few quarters; you have to plug a meter for parking. Don't be surprised if walkers have been in the ski tracks before you.

Information
UMD Outdoor Program, 121 SpHC, 10 University Drive, Duluth MN 55812, (218) 726-6533.
www.UMDrsop.org

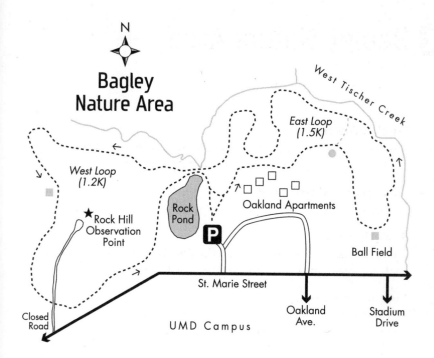

Bagley
Nature Area

WEST LOOP (1.2K)

Intermediate. This is the more challenging of the two loops as
you ski around Rock Hill, a former downhill ski area. The trail
climbs for a long time through maple forest with some nice
paper birch mixed in. Where the trail crosses a closed road to
the top of Rock Hill, stop for some winter tree identification:
there is maple, oak and basswood here—can you pick them out?
A downhill run takes you back to Rock Pond.

EAST LOOP (1.5K)

Intermediate. Take a quick loop through UMD's maple sugar-
bush. This is mostly level terrain except for a steep section along
Tischer Creek, where you will need to herringbone or sidestep.
You can bypass this difficult section on a skier-groomed cutoff.

Snowflake Nordic Center

Duluth, Minnesota

Trailhead access
Take Rice Lake Road 0.5 mile north of Arrowhead Road.
Entrance road is shared with tennis club.

Total groomed trail: 15K
Classical skiing: 15K   Skate skiing: 15K   Lighted trail: 6K

Pass requirements
• Day passes ($7; $3 after 5pm or for kids 5-12). Season passes
have a steep preseason discount. The policy is "All Olympians
ski free," and you actually may find some Winter Games
competitors here.

Trail difficulty
Generally intermediate terrain, though trail builders took
advantage of a few steep hills. The hardest part might be finding
a parking spot on busy afternoons and weekends.

Trailhead facilities
Chalet with restrooms, changing rooms, sauna, and wax room.
Rentals, kid and adult lessons, beverages and snacks available.

What makes it unique
Thanks to the boundless energy of the legendary George
Hovland, Snowflake provides high-quality grooming and facilities
right in town. Hovland was on the 1952 Oslo Olympics ski
team, and he's still out on the trails. When conditions are
marginal, your best bet for good skiing in Duluth is here.
Snowflake is frequented by ski racers and hosts the local high
school ski teams for practices as well as races. Sundays can get
busy with kid ski programs, skijor races and more.

Information
Snowflake Nordic Center, 4348 Rice Lake Road, Duluth MN
55811, (218) 726-1550. www.skiduluth.com

Snowflake Nordic Center

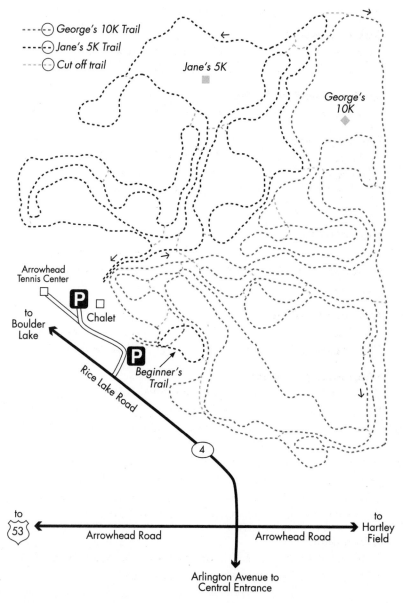

--⊙-- George's 10K Trail
--⊙-- Jane's 5K Trail
--⊙-- Cut off trail

Jane's 5K

George's
10K

Arrowhead
Tennis Center

🅿

Chalet

to
Boulder
Lake

🅿

Rice Lake Road

Beginner's
Trail

④

to
⑤③

Arrowhead Road   Arrowhead Road

to
Hartley
Field

Arlington Avenue to
Central Entrance

JANE'S 5K (5K)

Intermediate/lighted. This loop is trickiest at the start and finish, with some short, steep climbs to challenge any skier. However, the middle "half" is relatively flat, with the main challenge coming from tight curves—this is a nice stretch to focus on technique. The lighting is effective if a little unromantic, with power lines strung from tree to tree. Ignore the other lights and trails and settle in for the curvy "here and now."

GEORGE'S 10K (10K)

Advanced. If you're into getting from Point A to Point B, this trail is not for you and might in fact drive you a bit crazy. But if you're into the aesthetics of a well-groomed trail and a well-designed curve, check this out. Don't even try to keep your bearings. This loop squeezes a great variety of terrain out of a tight area, beginning with some steep ups and downs. If the first hills intimidated you, hold on; you've made it through the only truly advanced stretch of the loop. The rest is classic intermediate terrain and leads eventually into some nice woods, both birch and evergreen. Various cutoffs let you trim the distance if you'd like.

COME NORTH, SKI LOVERS

Compared to the Twin Cities, the North Shore is skiers' heaven. Sure, an early storm might go south and bring city-dwellers a few days of great skiing. But week after week, the most reliable snow and skiing conditions in Minnesota are on the Shore. Duluth has 109 days per winter with at least 6 inches of snow, and Grand Marais has 94; Minneapolis has just 54. Around the Flathorn-Gegoka trails, there's over 90 days a year with snow over 12 inches deep; Saint Paul averages 20 days a year with snow like that. Every 5 miles north on I-35 brings an additional inch of average snow per year.

Boulder Lake

Duluth, Minnesota

Trailhead access
Boulder Lake is 18 miles north of Duluth. Take Highway 4 north past Island Lake, then turn left on Boulder Dam Road. There are three trailheads along Boulder Dam Road: Large and popular **(1) Bear Paw/Blue Ox trailhead,** with its intermediate trails; Smaller and quieter **(2) North Parking Lot trailhead** by Nordberg Road, with advanced trails; Smallest and quietest **(3) Dam Parking Lot trailhead** at Boulder Dam, at the end of the road, with the easy Otter Run trail. All trails are connected.

Total groomed trail: 19.2K
Classical skiing: 19.2K   Skate skiing: 14.6

Trail difficulty
Each trailhead (see above) provides a different degree of difficulty.

Pass requirements
• None

Trailhead facilities
Outhouse at Rolling Pin and Otter Run trailheads. Wolfski's Ski Den warming shack has hot beverages, open dawn to dusk.

Snow conditions: (218) 721-4903

What makes it unique
These trails are built on a combination of land owned by Minnesota Power, the state, and the county near the shores of Boulder Lake, a reservoir for Minnesota Power's hydroelectric system. Readers of a local alternative paper, the *Reader Weekly,* voted these trails as the best place to ski in Duluth. On Sundays and Thursdays, leashed dogs are welcome on the trails.

Information
Boulder Lake Environmental Center (218) 721-3372. www.blma.org

ROLLING PIN/RIDGE RUNNER/TIMBER CRUISER (2.4K)

Intermediate to expert/classical only. These three trails form a figure eight using a glacial esker for the "cross." Because of the one-way markings, most skiers will ski all three. Rolling Pin winds you around to the start of Ridge Runner, which traces the top of an esker. Timber Cruiser starts with a big downhill ("Chiller Hill") coming off of the esker and runs through a recently logged area.

OTTER RUN (2.4K)

Beginner/classical only. This curvy loop trail is the easiest part of the system; with its own trailhead, it's perfect for a beginner. The forest is incredibly diverse here, with thick, old white pine at the western end, plus maple, large-toothed aspen and ash. The entire trail is level and easy going. Boulder Lake Reservoir drains into Island Lake through Otter Creek, thus the name of this trail. Beginners will want to access this loop from the parking lot at Boulder Dam to avoid the hills at the Rolling Pin trailhead.

BEAR PAW (2.3K)

Intermediate/skating and classical. Access this trail either from the Bear Paw/Blue Ox or Rolling Pin trailheads—the latter trailhead by heading across Boulder Lake itself at the warming hut, on a trail across the frozen lake (follow the trees stuck in the snow). This loop takes you through a young aspen forest with occasional patches of old white pine. A few easy hills make this barely an intermediate trail.

BLUE OX (3.8K)

Intermediate/skating and classical. Babe the Blue Ox was Paul Bunyan's helper in logging the mighty pines. This trail shows the "before" and "after" of Babe's work. The first half of this loop rolls gently through a wonderful white pine forest. The second half is all vigorous regrowth of aspen and birch. It's a good place to take an advanced beginner for his or her first big loop.

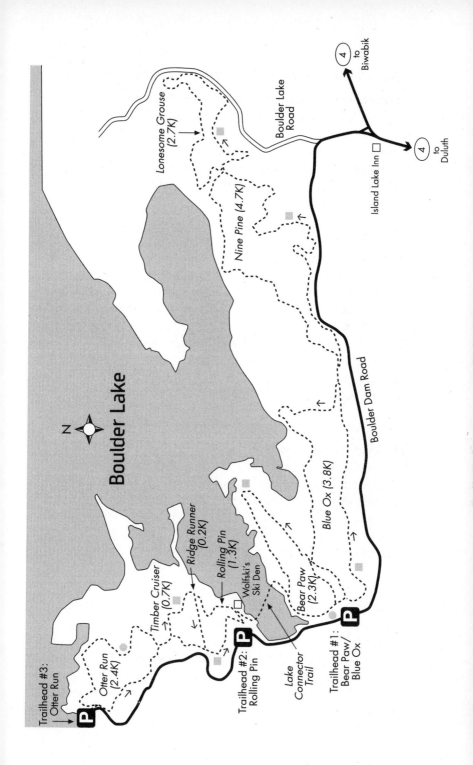

Boulder Lake

N

Trailhead #3: Otter Run

Trailhead #2: Rolling Pin

Trailhead #1: Bear Paw/Blue Ox

Lake Connector Trail

Wolfski's Ski Den

Otter Run (2.4K)

Timber Cruiser (0.7K)

Ridge Runner (0.2K)

Rolling Pin (1.3K)

Bear Paw (2.3K)

Blue Ox (3.8K)

Nine Pine (4.7K)

Lonesome Grouse (2.7K)

Boulder Lake Road

Boulder Dam Road

Island Lake Inn

4 to Biwabik

4 to Duluth

NINE PINE (4.7K)

Intermediate/skating and classical. If you enjoyed Blue Ox, cross the snowmobile trail and experience very similar terrain, with a few additional thrills and spills. The "Can of Nerves" takes you through a steep hairpin in a dark piney forest. Like Blue Ox, the northern half is mostly open, with a nice view at the overlook that supposedly lets you see nine pine trees.

LONESOME GROUSE (2.7K)

Intermediate/skating and classical. Really only a beginner trail through aspen and fir, but you have to be a good skier just to get out this far. While some folks in your party take a snack break at the shelter at the start, others can cruise this easy loop.

TRACKING BACKWARDS

Animals such as the snowshoe hare, deer mouse and red squirrel are hoppers, and their tracks show an unusual pattern. After an animal hops, it lands first on its front feet. Then its back feet come down in front of the front feet. The snowshoe hare track is found near areas with thick underbrush; the much smaller red squirrel track generally runs from tree to tree in coniferous forests. You can always tell which way a hopper was headed; just think backwards. ✳

Canosia Wildlife Management Area Trail

Town of Canosia, Minnesota

Trailhead access
2.5 miles north of Martin Road on Ugstad Road in Canosia
Township. Ugstad Road is 4.0 miles west of Rice Lake Road
on Martin Road.

Total groomed trail: 4.5K
Classical skiing: 4.5K

Trail difficulty
The first loop is especially nice and easy, once you get out of
the parking lot. Watch for moose.

Pass requirements
• None

Trailhead facilities
None

What makes it unique
This is a level, easy trail with terrific views of surrounding
wetlands. The Canosia State Wildlife Management Area has a
huge artificial wetland at its core, created primarily for
waterfowl habitat.

Information
Canosia State Wildlife Management Area, Minnesota DNR,
4805 Rice Lake Road, Duluth MN 55803.

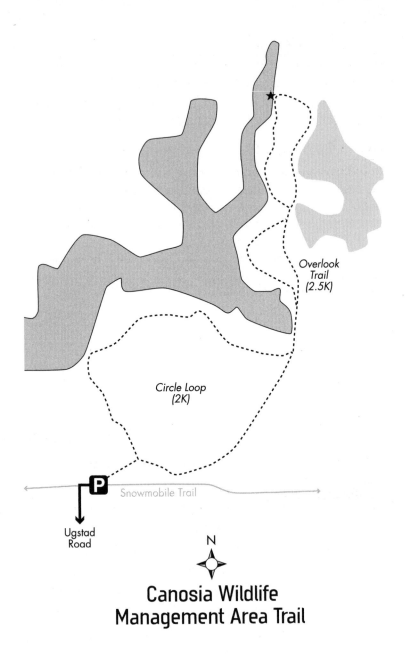

Overlook
Trail
(2.5K)

Circle Loop
(2K)

P

Snowmobile Trail

Ugstad
Road

N

Canosia Wildlife
Management Area Trail

CIRCLE LOOP (2K)

Easier. A nice mostly level loop through a scrubby but diverse forest of aspen, birch and balsam fir. You might have to climb one small bump. To summer hikers, this is known as the Angell Pool Trail. Nice views on the northern half out to the marsh.

OVERLOOK TRAIL (2.5K)

Intermediate. Two lollipop loops make for a stretched-out figure-eight after crossing an earthen dam that holds in the marshes. The woods here are a bit more diverse and the trail a bit more challenging than the Circle Loop. Be sure to stop at the last overlook, located on a rise with a great view of the marsh; it's especially scenic at dusk. The western or left side of the loops is easier than the eastern or right side. This trail is also labeled as the Burnt Ridge Trail.

THE NORTH SHORE WEATHER-GO-ROUND

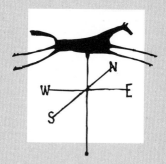

The weather in this region changes on cycles of 3–4 days. That means if you are here for just a short weekend, you might not see much change. If you spend a week on the North Shore, you will see whole weather systems moving in and out. Grey, 20-degree days turn into snowy days, followed by northwest winds bringing frigid air and clear skies from the Arctic. And then it starts all over again. ❄

Korkki Nordic Ski Center

Duluth, Minnesota

Trailhead access
Take Homestead Road (County Road 42) 2.5 miles north from milepost 14.9 on Highway 61 expressway, to left turn at Korkki Road. Go west on Korkki Road (County Road 43) for 0.5 miles to Nordic Center entrance on right.

Total groomed trail: 11K
Classical skiing: 11K

Trail difficulty
Korkki Nordic is challenging terrain, but the hills and curves are so well laid out you feel more thrilled than scared.

Pass requirements
• None. Donation box at trailhead. Suggested donation of $3–$5. Korkki Nordic Ski Center was formed as a nonprofit organization dedicated to maintaining this premiere example of traditional Nordic skiing. Annual memberships encouraged ($15/family, $10 individual).

Trailhead facilities
Chalet with wood stove and changing room. Outhouse.

Snow conditions: (218) 525-7326

What makes it unique
These are truly "Charlie's Trails," as they are affectionately called by those in the know. Charlie Banks was one of the legendary figures of Duluth skiing, and built these trails himself in 1955 on public land in his "backyard." The club maintains the trail and its history and character, preserving traditional single-track, classical skiing and a sense of skiing community. Korkki Nordic has been called "possibly the prettiest trail on the North Shore."

Information
Korkki Nordic, 1711 Korkki Road, Duluth MN 55804.

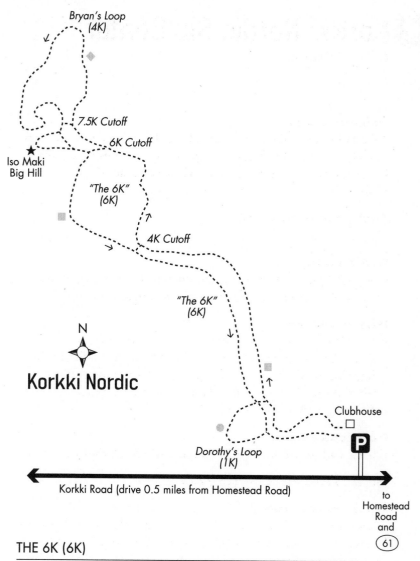

Bryan's Loop
(4K)

7.5K Cutoff

6K Cutoff

Iso Maki
Big Hill

"The 6K"
(6K)

4K Cutoff

"The 6K"
(6K)

N

Korkki Nordic

Clubhouse

P

Dorothy's Loop
(1K)

Korkki Road (drive 0.5 miles from Homestead Road)

to
Homestead
Road
and
(61)

THE 6K (6K)

Intermediate. This is single-tracked and narrow, with exciting hills where you can't see the bottom and throw caution to the wind...but it all works out fine. You gradually climb through mixed forest and ash swamps, then return on a wonderful gradual downhill run that makes you feel like a champion skier. There are two especially challenging parts of the downhill run, where the trail goes down and back up along a river bank. Most skiers stay on the main trail through these features, but beginning skiers can avoid these more difficult sections on side trails.

BRYAN'S LOOP (4K)

Advanced. Skiers choosing the "whole enchilada" will experience more challenging terrain, with some sharp turns on steep hills. There are some nice beaver ponds and piney ridges (known as "Wolf Kill Ridge") back here, too. The middle third of the loop is relatively level and in open woods, but the last third has a hairpin turn and other thrills. The "Iso Maki Big Hill," also available to those who take the 7.5K cutoff, is a steep climb to a great view from the top of inland ridges, and a speedy run down a hill that seems to go on forever. A cutoff is available to those who want to skip the hill.

DOROTHY'S LOOP (1K)

Easier. This recently added loop, flatter and wider than the main loop, is perfect for kids and instructional outings, except you have to take the first swooping hill to get there. Real beginners should ski the loop clockwise.

Mother Bear Ski Trail

Brimson, Minnesota

Trailhead access

On St. Louis County Road 44, 2 miles SW of Brimson and 9 miles NE of Pequaywan Lakes (about 35 miles from eastern Duluth or about a 1-hour drive). From Korkki Nordic and Highway 61, it's a fun and winding 40-minute drive along county roads 42, 41, and 266 to 44.

Total groomed trail: 10.7 K

Classical skiing: 10.7K

Trail difficulty

Stay in the first set of loops and it's pretty easy terrain. Out on the remote western loops, the trail gets trickier and fewer people ski there, so be extra careful.

Pass requirements

• None, though donations may be sent to Mother Bear Ski Trail, 1398 Camp House Road, Brimson, MN, 55602. Membership is $10 per year, per family. Membership forms available at trailhead.

Trailhead facilities

Outhouse

What makes it unique

Off the beaten path, this trail primarily serves local residents. Because this trail is not used as often as others, and because the forest is so varied here, the animal tracking can be superb. Watch for signs of wolf, lynx and snowshoe hare, especially on the South Loop.

Information

Mother Bear Ski Trail, 1398 Camp House Road, Brimson MN 55602.

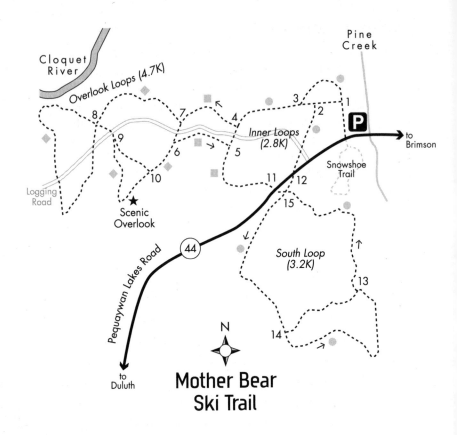

INNER LOOPS (2.8K)

Easy to difficult. These are intersections marked 1–5. From marker 1 counterclockwise around past 2 and 3 to 4, it's a gradual run through a variety of conifers and then an open area. Beginners should turn around at marker 4 and retrace their tracks, as the trail to marker 15 takes some steep downhill turns without much room to snowplow.

SOUTH LOOP (3.2K)

Easy. A longer, gentle loop through nice pine forest, with a more challenging side trail from 14 to 13. You have to cross the highway to get to these trails, but it's worth the effort.

OVERLOOK LOOPS (4.7K)

Expert. This is a series of loops with nice views, crisscrossing a logging road. Most of the loops are one-way counterclockwise. You can take just one or do all three. The 4-7-6-5 loop starts with a big climb through young aspen and ends with a fun, tricky downhill. Only adventurous skiers should attempt the curvy, skier-groomed trail from 7 to 8. The 6-10-9 loop runs through a boggy area and on top of what appears to be a glacial esker. The last 1.6K loop starts and ends at 8 and leads to an overlook of the Cloquet River and the edge of a rim overlooking a spruce bog below.

TRACKS OF THE LONG AND LEAN

The North Woods have many long and lean members of the weasel family, and they all leave a distinctive track pattern, a pair of prints nearly side by side but slightly offset. Each set of tracks is between one and three feet away from the next, representing the "bound" of the sinuous animals. This is actually a running gait, with the front feet landing first and the rear feet landing exactly in the prints left by the front feet.

The two most common weasels leaving tracks by your ski trail are the pine marten and the fisher. The animals are similar enough in size that their tracks are hard to tell apart; a smaller footprint (just less than two inches long) would be a marten and a larger set (just slightly more than two inches long) would be a fisher, but there's lots of room in between. Use habitat as a clue: marten are found in the mature boreal forest where they can chase squirrels through the trees. The fisher often captures porcupine and prefers a more open successional forest. ❄

Lake County

State parks and local volunteers: skiing Lake County gives you new appreciation of both. The North Shore state parks stand out on the maps, from the diverse trail network at Gooseberry to the deep woods and dramatic terrain of Tettegouche. But you'll also find some gems tucked into the hills, like Silver Bay's Northwoods Ski Touring Trail and the Erkki Harju Ski Trail, both maintained by local volunteers. Away from the shore, on the edge of the Boundary Waters, explore the deep snow and towering pines of Flathorn-Gegoka. Maybe they should change Lake County's name to "Snow County!"

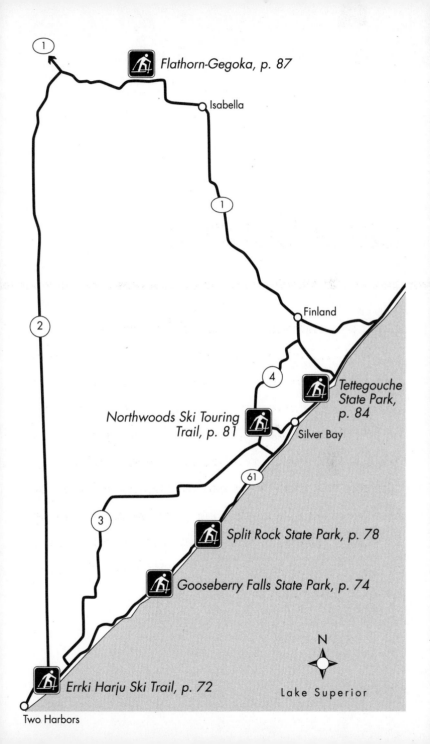

Flathorn-Gegoka, p. 87

Isabella

Finland

Tettegouche
State Park,
p. 84

Northwoods Ski Touring
Trail, p. 81

Silver Bay

Split Rock State Park, p. 78

Gooseberry Falls State Park, p. 74

N

Errki Harju Ski Trail, p. 72

Lake Superior

Two Harbors

Erkki Harju Ski Trail

Two Harbors, Minnesota

Trailhead access
Take County Road 2 from Highway 61 north 0.7 miles until signed entrance to parking lot on the right side of the road.

Total groomed trail: 9K
Classical skiing: 9K   Skate skiing: 9K

Trail difficulty
These are mostly easier trails, but with a few optional side loops that add some spice.

Pass requirements
• Great Minnesota Ski Pass
• Membership in Two Harbors Ski Club recommended ($10/individual, $15/family).

Trailhead facilities
None

What makes it unique
Also known as the Two Harbors Ski Rec Trail, this is a gentle, quiet set of ski trails well used and loved by local families and the high school team. The 3K inside loop is the only lighted trail between Duluth and Grand Marais.

Information
Two Harbors Ski Club, PO Box 381, Two Harbors MN 55616.

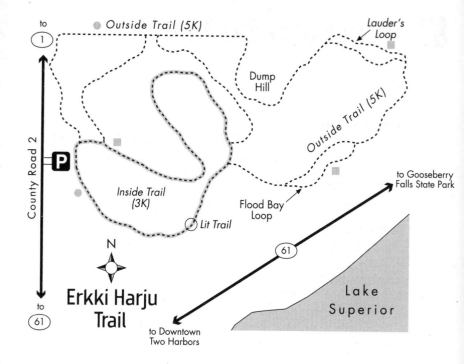

INSIDE TRAIL (3K)

Intermediate/lighted. This inside loop forms the outline of a "C" as it runs through the strips of woods between the fairways of Lakeview National Golf Course. The open fairways provide an airy feel to your ski. The lights look like little lighthouses and are actually airstrip runway lights.

OUTSIDE TRAIL (5K, plus 1K advanced side loops)

Easier to advanced. The terrain is gently rolling, with few uphills or downhills. This trail leaves the fairways behind. Two side loops of about 0.5K each, the Flood Bay Loop and Lauder's Loop, are for advanced skiers, with quick turns and sharp climbs. Between the two side trails is an ungroomed connector trail leading to Superior Shores resort. Toward the end of the loop, once you have your bearings, you can weave between the 3K and the 5K loops before finishing back at the trailhead.

Gooseberry Falls State Park

Two Harbors, Minnesota

Trailhead access

Take Visitor Center/Wayside Rest exit off Highway 61, twelve miles northeast of Two Harbors. Go either to Visitor Center or to Lakeview picnic shelter on lakeshore.

Total groomed trail: 20K

Classical skiing: 20K

Trail difficulty

If the snow is good, beginners can stay on the lake side of the highway. Getting to the rest of the trail system is tricky but very rewarding.

Pass Requirements

- Great Minnesota Ski Pass (self-service permits available in Visitor Center)
- Minnesota State Parks vehicle permit (only when using Lakeview picnic center trailhead)

Trailhead facilities

Restrooms, snacks, warming room, gift shop and Visitor Center.

What makes it unique

Gooseberry is the first big North Shore ski area as you head up the shore. Its diverse terrain and remote trails make it a favorite for day trippers from the Duluth area. Families with young children can use the beautiful lobby of the visitor center as a warming hut—and parents can take turns exploring the trails.

Information

Gooseberry Falls State Park, 1300 Highway 61,
Two Harbors MN 55616, (218) 834-3855.
www.dnr.state.mn.us/state_parks/gooseberry_falls

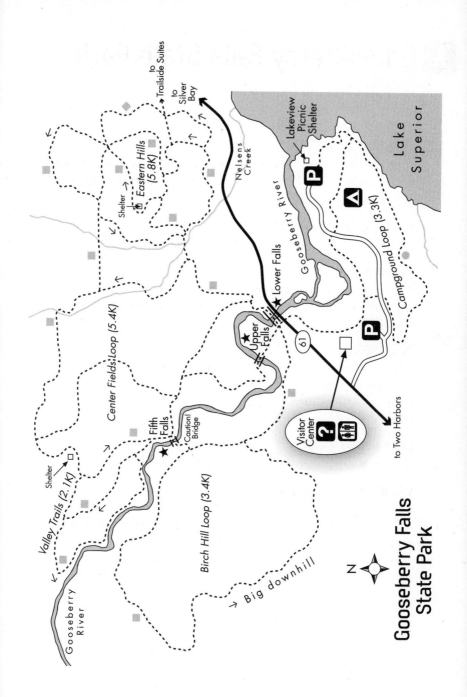

Gooseberry Falls
State Park

N

to Trailside Suites
to Silver Bay

Lake Superior

Lakeview Picnic Shelter

P

Campground Loop (3.3K)

Nelsens Creek

Gooseberry River

Lower Falls

Upper Falls

Eastern Hills (5.8K)

Shelter

Center Fields Loop (5.4K)

Fifth Falls

Cautionl Bridge

Valley Trails (2.1K)

Shelter

Birch Hill Loop (3.4K)

Big downhill

Gooseberry River

61

P

Visitor Center ? ♿

to Two Harbors

CAMPGROUND LOOP (3.3K)

Easy. Take this trail either direction through the open woods of the lakeshore and campground area. You can start from the Visitor Center area, or if you have a vehicle permit you can start on the 0.3K spur from Lakeview picnic shelter by Agate Beach. The views of the Gooseberry River valley and the icy Lake Superior shore are among the most dramatic of all North Shore trails. The trail crosses a park road twice, so you may have to take off your skis or step gingerly across the pavement.

Inland trails

Access these trails from the Visitor Center. A busy main feeder trail parallels a snowmobile trail under the highway bridge on the west side of river, with a dramatic view of the Upper Falls.

BIRCH HILL LOOP (3.4K)

More difficult. After crossing under Highway 61, you will take a 0.7K access trail to this remote loop. Watch for the deer exclosure just past the junction with the trail down to Fifth Falls. After a steep climb to the open ridgeline, get ready for a fun, gradual 1.2K downhill run. When you finally have to kick again, it will be in a nice mixed open forest. Use caution as you near the highway, as the trail is shared with snowmobiles and the last turn down to the bridge is tricky.

CENTER FIELDS LOOP (5.4K)

More difficult. Cross the groovy bridge over the Gooseberry River and under the highway. Or head up the Birch Hill loop and cross the river on a snowmobile bridge. This is open country of spruce and birch. The main counterclockwise loop is 4.4K of trail from the bridge. It's great for relaxed cruising, especially on a sunny day when you can stop at the shelter and bask in the rays. The two-way cutoff up the middle of the loop adds variety. Take off from this main loop onto either of the sections below for a full adventure. Enjoy a break at the Fifth Falls bridge, or use the bridge to reach the Birch Hill Loop, but do take off your skis before heading down.

VALLEY TRAILS (2.1K)

More difficult. If the skiing is fast, this section can be scary and should be rated most difficult. Downhill runs come off the Center Fields loop and scoot you down to the banks of the Gooseberry, where you will cruise past some huge cedar trees. The climb back up the river bank is fairly long and steep.

EASTERN HILLS (5.8K)

More difficult to most difficult. Head out into this section, and if you are comfortable with some hills and turns, forget about the maps that show up every few hundred meters and just follow your curiosity up and down and around these hills. You won't get lost, but you will enjoy open country of birch and spruce. One 0.8K section is rated advanced for its tight turns and sharp hills; it also connects with an ungroomed trail to a neighboring lodge. If you make it to the shelter, pull out a snack and enjoy the view!

> ## GOOSEBERRY TRAILSIDE SUITES
>
> With direct access to the eastern trails, this unique lodging property has just four suites, tucked into quiet woods. Visit www.gooseberry.com or call (800) 715-1110.

WARMER BY THE LAKE? REALLY?

Some folks call the North Shore the "Norwegian Riviera." Believe it or not, North Shore communities can be the warmest places in Minnesota when it's really cold statewide. Lake Superior has an average temperature of 39 degrees Fahrenheit. In summer, the lake acts like a big ice cube and keeps us cool; in winter, it acts like a big radiator and keeps us warm. ❄

Split Rock Lighthouse State Park

Two Harbors, Minnesota

Trailhead access

Go to Split Rock Lighthouse State Park, 21 miles northeast of Two Harbors on Highway 61. Follow signs to the right past the guard station to parking lot at Trail Center.

Total groomed trail: 12.8K

Classical skiing: 12.8K

Trail difficulty

Tight turns and narrow trails make this area challenging. You might wish you were wearing snowshoes instead.

Pass Requirements

• Great Minnesota Ski Pass
• Minnesota State Parks vehicle permit

Trailhead facilities

Trail Center with restrooms and indoor picnic facility.

What makes it unique

Having the trails right along the Lake Superior shore adds drama and beauty to your ski. The Trail Center provides a great base for a winter day in the park.

Information

Split Rock Lighthouse State Park, 2010A Highway 61 East, Two Harbors MN 55616, (218) 226-6377.
www.dnr.state.mn.us/state_parks/split_rock_lighthouse

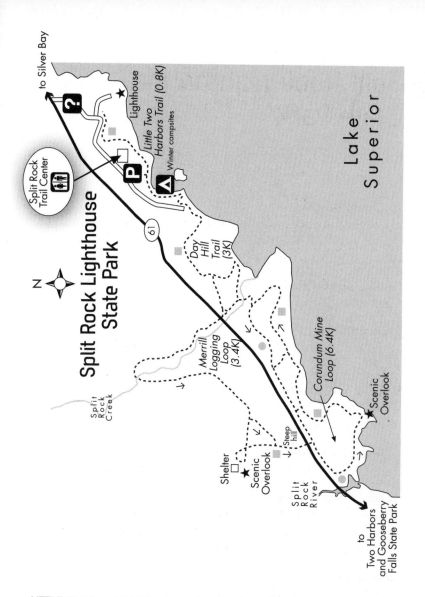

LITTLE TWO HARBORS AND DAY HILL TRAILS (3.2K)

Intermediate. Your introduction to skiing at Split Rock includes both essential elements of this park's trails: lakeshore skiing and speedy hills. Starting from the Trail Center you can either head up the Gitchi Gami Trail toward the lighthouse or ski around Day Hill, climbing over 100 feet to get to the rest of the trail system. A 1.6K loop takes you to a nice view west. Coming back, the view of the lighthouse from Little Two Harbors, where the ski trail is right on the cobblestone beach, is postcard perfect.

CORUNDUM MINE LOOP (6.4K)

Intermediate. Much of outbound part of this loop follows the old highway, providing smooth skiing at first. Coming back along the lakeshore is a little more exciting, especially with less deep snow near the shore. Since the trail is regularly packed and groomed, it stays in pretty good shape.

MERRILL LOGGING LOOP (3.4K)

Intermediate. After carefully crossing Highway 61, you will climb the eastern bank of Split Rock Creek. The climb takes you past a large deer exclosure to a junction with the Superior Hiking Trail and then quickly onto the bed of an old logging railroad. This provides a straight shot down for 1K before climbing steeply to a shelter and overlook with a nice view down to the Split Rock River, Highway 61 and Lake Superior.

LAKE SUPERIOR ICE IS NICE

February and March are the best months for ice watchers. The water of Lake Superior is at its coldest in the month of March. Almost every year the shallower or more protected bays of the North Shore will freeze over during the late winter, but some years it is frozen as far as the eye can see. And once every twenty years or so, the whole lake freezes over—which takes a combination of a long-term cold winter, a serious cold snap and relatively calm seas, which is what happened in 1978 and 1994. However, climate change experts say we may never see a full freeze again. ❄

Northwoods Ski Touring Trail
Silver Bay, Minnesota

Trailhead access
Take Outer Drive, which becomes Penn Boulevard and Superior National Forest Scenic Byway, through the town of Silver Bay for a total of 3.2 miles from Highway 61 (past a parking area for the Superior Hiking Trail) to signed parking area on right.

Total groomed trail: 19K
Classical skiing: 19K

Trail difficulty
With the narrow trails and some hills on every loop, this is not a beginner trail system. Check it out for yourself!

Pass Requirements
• Great Minnesota Ski Pass
• Recommended annual membership in club ($10/family, $5/individual) or use donation box at trailhead.

Trailhead facilities
None

What makes it unique
This local trail adds a traditional twist to North Shore skiing. The narrow trails and great views make this feel like you are on the Superior Hiking Trail. Bean Lake is a favorite destination for hikers in the summer and skiers in the winter.

Information
Northwoods Ski Touring Club, Box 52, Silver Bay MN 55614, (218) 226-4334.

MAPLE CORNER LOOPS (3.3K)

Easier. These beginner loops quickly immerse you in the intimacy of this trail system as you climb along the banks of the east branch of the Beaver River. Be sure to sign in at the trail register…and check out the colorful comments of your fellow skiers. It's 2.8K around the outside loop and 2.1K around the inside loop. Use caution on the two snowmobile trail crossings. There are fun but easy downhill runs with mountain-like views.

BIG PINE CORNER LOOP (4.7K)

Intermediate to advanced. This trail weaves up the open country of the Beaver River and its tributary, Smokey Creek, to Big Pine Corner, crisscrossing a snowmobile trail then turning south. From there you can either huff it over Herringbone Hill, 0.9K of a big up and down, or continue on a more level trail.

POPLAR/SPRUCE/BALSAM CORNERS (3.9K)

Intermediate to Advanced. The side trails and scenic loop are for advanced skiers. Either climb up from Poplar Corner to the panoramic views from the scenic overlook or descend from Spruce Corner into the rolling hillside.

BEAN LAKE SPUR (1.1K)

Intermediate. Ski in either around or across (from Poplar Corner) a large beaver pond into the rugged territory of Bean Lake. Three different trails converge at the same place on the lake, so be careful on your way back that you choose the right one.

TETTEGOUCHE CONNECTOR (6K)

Intermediate. Because of the distance involved and the remoteness, this section should only be skied by experienced, prepared skiers. After crossing Smokey Creek, the trail follows the creek's upper reaches in a valley which gets narrower and narrower until you pass through a gorge with 250-foot sides. The last few kilometers before Tettegouche Camp get pretty rough since they are on state park hiking trails and are hard to groom.

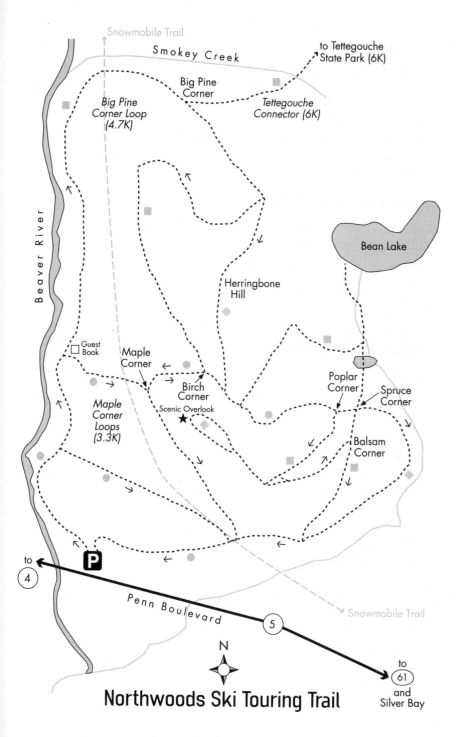

Snowmobile Trail

Smokey Creek

to Tettegouche
State Park (6K)

Big Pine
Corner

Big Pine
Corner Loop
(4.7K)

Tettegouche
Connector (6K)

Beaver River

Bean Lake

Herringbone
Hill

Guest
Book

Maple
Corner

Birch
Corner

Poplar
Corner

Spruce
Corner

Scenic Overlook

Maple
Corner
Loops
(3.3K)

Balsam
Corner

to
4

P

Penn Boulevard

5

Snowmobile Trail

N

to
61
and
Silver Bay

Northwoods Ski Touring Trail

Tettegouche State Park

Silver Bay, Minnesota

Trailhead access
Take Highway 61 four miles northeast of Silver Bay to park entrance. With a state park vehicle permit, head up park access road to parking lot at trailhead.

Total groomed trail: 13.5K
Classical skiing: 13.5K   Skate skiing: 7.5K

Trail difficulty
Every trail here has some sort of screaming downhill, but trails are groomed wide enough to keep it fairly safe.

Pass requirements
• Great Minnesota Ski Pass
• Minnesota State Parks vehicle permit

Trailhead facilities
Outhouses

What makes it unique
Long loops into quiet, dramatic country make for a real sense of adventure. The restored log cabins of Tettegouche Camp provide a unique ski-in overnight adventure deep inside the park.

Information
Tettegouche State Park, 5702 Highway 61, Silver Bay MN 55614, (218) 226-6365. www.dnr.state.mn.us/state_parks/tettegouche

TETTEGOUCHE CAMP CABINS

Tettegouche State Park offers rustic, ski-in only lodging in four log cabins. Reservations are available up to one year in advance. Visit www.dnr.state.mn.us/state_parks/tettegouche for more information; call 866-85PARKS or visit www.stayatmnparks for cabin reservations.

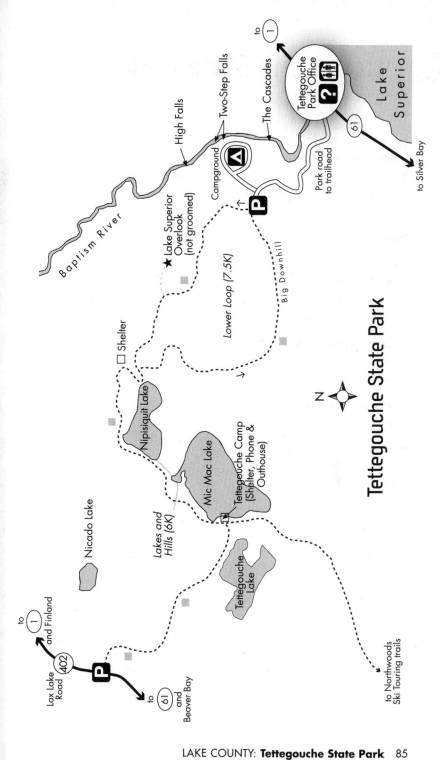

Tettegouche State Park

Lake Superior

Baptism River

to 1

Tettegouche Park Office

2

Park road to trailhead

61

to Silver Bay

High Falls

Two-Step Falls

The Cascades

Campground

Lake Superior Overlook (not groomed)

Lower Loop (7.5K)

Big Downhill

Shelter

N

Nipisiquit Lake

Nicado Lake

Lakes and Hills (6K)

Mic Mac Lake

Tettegouche Camp (Shelter, Phone & Outhouse)

Tettegouche Lake

to 1 and Finland

Lax Lake Road 402

to 61 and Beaver Bay

to Northwoods Ski Touring trails

LOWER LOOP (7.5K)

Intermediate/skating and classical. This is a classic North Shore ski outing, where you will climb through a variety of habitats, then enjoy a thrilling downhill run back to the trailhead. Throw into the mix a nice inland lake, big old trees and almost 5K of skiing without an intersection to think about. The 2.9K climb to Nipisiquit Lake is nice enough, with a mix of younger forest and the opportunity to hack your way up to the Lake Superior overlook (this spur trail is not groomed). Nipisiquit Lake will take what's left of your breath away, and on a sunny afternoon the picnic spot there will tempt you to stay awhile. The trail back from Nipisiquit continues to climb past some wonderful yellow birch. Shortly after you cross the Superior Hiking Trail, on a fast day you will head downhill, with enough speed you will wish you had goggles.

LAKES AND HILLS (6K)

Intermediate and advanced. Watch for signs of wolf as you skirt the hills and lake shores of this rugged terrain on the classical-only trail. After rounding Papasay Ridge, you will be back on Nipisiquit Lake. This may tempt you to ski across the ice on your way back, but do so only with extreme caution, especially near the streams that empty out of or into the lake. Mic Mac and Tettegouche Lakes are next. If you haven't made your reservation at the cabins on Mic Mac, you will want to do so for next year once you see them. Just for kicks, use the pay phone to call home. The trail in from the parking lot on Lax Lake Road (Lake County Road 402) is a wide road and can be skated, but is steep enough to keep its intermediate ranking or even be considered advanced.

TETTEGOUCHE CONNECTOR

See entry for the Northwoods Ski Touring Trail (p. 82).

Flathorn-Gegoka

Isabella, Minnesota

Trailhead access
Take Highway 1 six miles west of Isabella and about 30 miles from Highway 61 to Mitiwan Lake Road. (Forest Road 177). Approximately 0.8 mile to trailhead on Flathorn Lake. The Lake Gegoka boat landing may also be plowed; from there you can cross the lake to intersection 3.

Total groomed trail: 27.6K
Classical skiing: 27.6K

Trail difficulty
Most of these trails are on old roads, so they're fairly level. Off on some of the connector routes or around Flathorn Lake, trails get narrower and trickier.

Pass Requirements
• Great Minnesota Ski Pass

Trailhead facilities
Outhouse. Full services at National Forest Lodge, available only to registered guests.

What makes it unique
These trails are ideally suited for overnight guests at National Forest Lodge. The beautiful white pine forest here is the result of humans and nature working together. Selective cutting has allowed pines to grow bigger and stronger.

NATIONAL FOREST LODGE

National Forest Lodge provides the ideal base camp for this vast system of remote trails. Stay in modest cabins and share family-style meals, then ski from your door out into the pines and lake-effect snow. Visit www.nationalforestlodge.com or call (651) 351-0939 for information and reservations.

Information
National Forest Lodge, 3226 Highway 1, Isabella MN 55607, (651-351-0939). www.nationalforestlodge.com

Flathorn-Gegoka

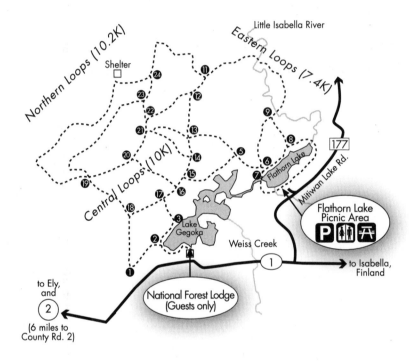

EASTERN LOOPS (7.4K) — Intersections 5–13

Intermediate. Entering trail system from the public access parking, you first ski around Flathorn Lake on challenging trails. Two crossings of the Little Isabella River are especially pretty. Between intersections 9 and 11 the narrow winding trail joins an old road and becomes straighter and flatter all the way to intersection 13. The trail from 5 to 6 and from 6 to 9 is rated most difficult and has steep curvy hills.

CENTRAL LOOPS (10K) — Intersections 1–3, 12–22

Easiest. These loops are the main set of trails for guests of National Forest Lodge. They offer tremendous variety among the big pines on a combination of old forest roads. East–west connector routes provide beautiful and more challenging skiing through black spruce bogs and cedar swamps.

NORTHERN LOOPS (10.2K) — Intersections 11, 19–24

Intermediate to most difficult. Move out of the white pine into the realm of red pine. These are all narrow winding trails and may be the last to be groomed. Spruce bogs complete the coniferous diversity. A shelter west of intersection 24 is a good lunch destination for a day-long outing on the northern loops.

NORTH SHORE SNOWBELTS: GO, SNOW, GO!

Want huge amounts of fresh, fluffy snow? Then hope for a southeast wind. Although rare, the southeast wind draws moisture from the open lake. When that moist air reaches land, the cold of the land mass and the height of the hills draw out the moisture—and it snows like crazy, especially along the ridgeline and inland toward Isabella, Minnesota. So-called "lake-effect snow" can dump up to five feet of snow, as it did in 1994 in the Silver Bay-Finland area. ❄

North Shore Mountains

Have you ever put on your skis and had such a good time you didn't want to stop? Here you don't have to stop. Over 200K of interconnected trails await, linking Carlton Peak to the Bally Creek trails, nearly to Grand Marais. The well-maintained trails weave in and out of the Sawtooth Mountains, connecting to tasteful lodges and B&Bs along the way. From Carlton Peak to the Cascade River the trails are groomed 10 to 15 feet wide by Pisten-Bully groomers. At the eastern end, the slightly more wild trails of Cascade River State Park and Bally Creek await. While backcountry adventurers head out on the 25K Picnic Loop, families cruise the Cascade River trails. Don't stop 'til you get to the espresso!

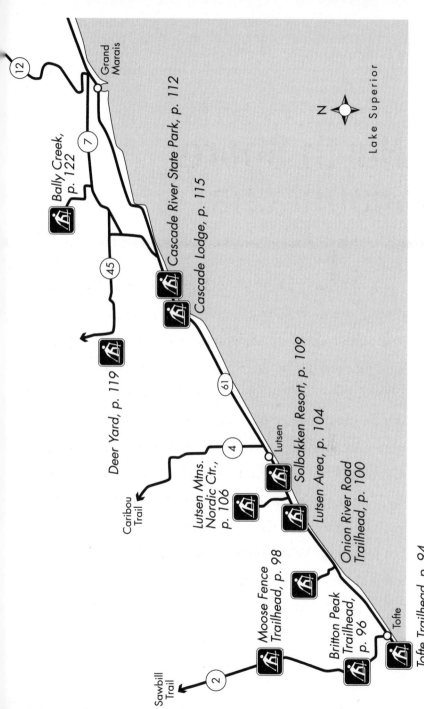

Sugarbush Trail System
Tofte, Minnesota

Trailhead access
(1) Tofte Trailhead: Take Tofte Homestead Road .2 miles from Highway 61 across from Bluefin Bay Resort. **(2) Britton Peak Trailhead:** Take Sawbill Trail 2.7 miles north of Tofte and Highway 61 to Britton Peak trailhead on right, with a large parking area at trailhead. **(3) Moose Fence Trailhead:** Take the Sawbill Trail 7.5 miles north of Highway 61 to a small, signed parking lot on right, directly off road. **(4) Onion River Road Trailhead:** Take Onion River Road (Forest Road 336) 2.1 miles north of Highway 61 to a large parking area on left, where the plowed road ends.

Total groomed trail: 69K
Classical skiing: 69K   Skate skiing: 69K

Trail difficulty
Beginning skiers might head for the Onion River Road or Moose Fence trailhead, while intermediate skiers will find their fill at Britton Peak.

Pass requirements
• Great Minnesota Ski Pass

Trailhead facilities
Outhouses at Britton Peak and Onion River Road trailheads; none at Moose Fence Trailhead.

Snow conditions: (800) 897-7669

What makes it unique
Excellent trails, easy access and proximity to resorts make this area a popular starting point for a North Shore ski vacation.

Information
Sugarbush Trail Association, PO Box 212, Tofte MN 55615. www.sugarbushtrail.org

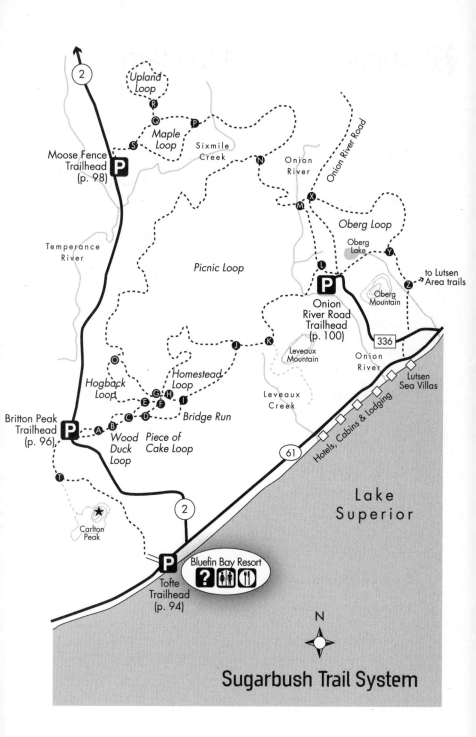

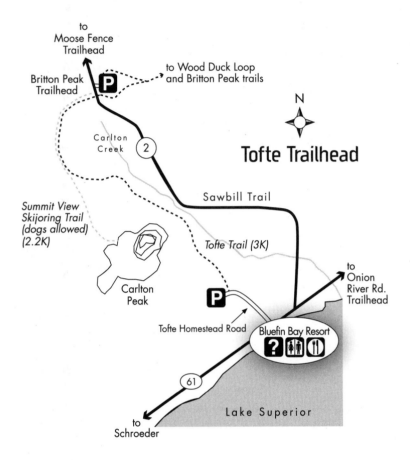

(1) Tofte Trailhead

These trails are useful for Tofte resort guests and for skiers with energetic dogs, including skijorers.

SUMMIT VIEW (2.2K)

Intermediate. Follow this summertime road up to the shoulder of Carlton Peak. The trail initially takes you through mostly open country before leading you to the base of the peak. From here you could change to snowshoes and hop on the Superior Hiking Trail to the summit.

TOFTE TRAIL (3K)

Intermediate. This trail is best used for so-called "norpine" skiing. Get someone to drive you to the Britton Peak trailhead, then ski downhill back to the lake and the Bluefin Bay trailhead. This is a fun run through a mostly birch forest. Be sure to look off to your right in some of the open areas for a dramatic view of Carlton Peak and the quarry on its southeast "face."

LAKE SUPERIOR STORM WATCHING

Winter storms on Lake Superior provide one of the most humbling experiences around. In a major storm, the lake is so powerful and the gusts are so strong that you feel like dust in the wind.

To best experience a roaring northeaster, find a promontory that faces "up" the shore, i.e. northeast. Dress more warmly than you expect to dress—the wind chill could easily be many degrees below zero, and you will want to stay out in the blast for at least ten minutes. Stand in a secure area just close enough to the breaking waves that you can smell the water but not be doused by it, since shifting winds can blow you off your feet.

For great storm watching, try:

- Agate Beach and the picnic area at Gooseberry Falls State Park.

- Shovel Point at Tettegouche State Park (the 20-minute walk in will warm you up).

- Highway 61 parking area at Cascade River State Park.

- Duluth's Lakewalk and Canal Park area near the aerial lift bridge and ship canal piers.

- Stoney Point.

- Artist's Point and East Bay Beach, Grand Marais.

- The Bluefin Grille in Tofte, where you can sip coffee and watch the breakers for a slightly more sedate experience.

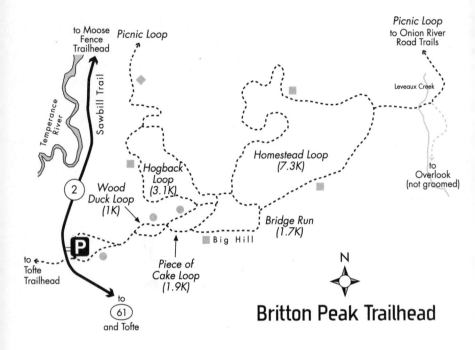

(2) Britton Peak Trailhead

The most popular trailhead on the North Shore, with good reason, this leads to great loop trails like the Homestead, Hogback and Picnic.

INNER LOOPS (WOOD DUCK & PIECE OF CAKE LOOPS) (2.9K)

Easiest. Entering the magnificent Sugarbush trails, these first loops are great for warm-ups or for introducing novices to the basics. Aggressive skiers will speed through these loops, but it's worth taking a few minutes to enjoy the views of Carlton Peak through the maples. Wood Duck Loop is named for a small pond it passes with a wood duck nesting box. True beginners should stay on the south part of the first loop to avoid a steep curve right before the parking lot.

HOGBACK LOOP (3.1K)

More difficult. If you are ready for a little more challenge, take the long climb up from the Piece of Cake Loop onto Hogback Ridge. This trail is two-way, but it's better skied clockwise. You'll leave the crowds behind and enjoy some challenging hills. There's one last climb after the junction with the Picnic Loop, then a long, gradual downhill to the end of the loop.

BRIDGE RUN (1.7K)

More difficult. This is a nice introduction to intermediate skiing, with a fast but straight downhill to kick off the loop (this is the two-way ski-through trail, so watch out for people coming the other way). The herringbone climb back up to the Piece of Cake Loop is challenging—but you will have more fun continuing around the Homestead Loop.

HOMESTEAD LOOP (7.3K)

More difficult. This makes a great half-day outing. As a counter-clockwise loop it saves the best for last: a 4.5K run through the maples with no stops or intersections, just great views of the Sawtooth mountains both up and down the shore, and two or three fun, short downhills to finish. There are nice lunch spots all along. Starting and ending at the Sawbill Trail, this makes for about a 12K ski.

PICNIC LOOP (25K TOTAL)

Most difficult. This is the classic North Shore ski adventure. The Picnic Loop is an annual ritual for many, a chance to immerse in the woods for an entire day while experiencing remote country on challenging trails. From the Britton Peak trailhead, it's at least 25K around, depending on which way you take the Homestead Loop. From the Onion River Road trailhead it's about 23K. The Picnic Loop incorporates parts of the Hogback and Homestead loops, and the Sixmile Crossing Trail but adds its own remote 9.2K. The downhill run after the junction with Sixmile Crossing Trail is an exciting set of switchbacks.

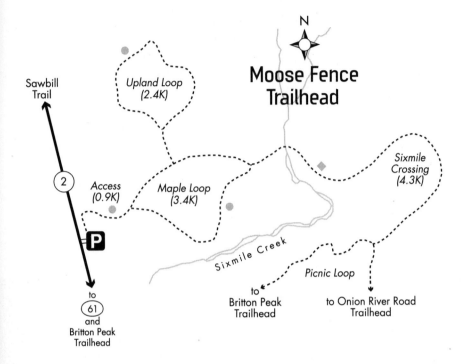

(3) Moose Fence Trailhead

Get away from the crowds but enjoy the same quality grooming and even deeper snow.

MAPLE LOOP (4.3K)

More difficult. A 0.9K access trail takes you from the trailhead up over a small ridge to the beginning of this loop. The hill down to the start of the loop is the biggest on the whole route. As the name implies, there is a lot of maple here, but there are also some nice open glades. Take the loop counterclockwise; the south side is a little hillier than the north, and you will climb about 150 feet, but none of it is steep.

UPLAND LOOP (2.4K)

Easiest. This is what is known as a "lollipop loop." The "stick" of the lollipop is the 0.4K two-way trail at the beginning. And the "candy" part of the lollipop really is sweet: almost 2K of level skiing on top of an easy ridge. Chances are you will want to ski this loop twice before heading back. Wildlife signs are common, including moose and a variety of birds.

SIXMILE CROSSING (4.3K)

Most difficult. This section of trail connects Moose Fence with the Picnic Loop and the main Sugarbush region. With a car shuttle, you can enjoy "norpine" skiing from the Moose Fence Trailhead down to the Onion River/Oberg Mountain trailhead. Notice the boreal spruce forest in the Sixmile Creek valley: cold air sinks from the maple ridges and keeps out the "riff-raff"—trees that can't survive temperatures below -40°F.

WHAT MOOSE? WHAT FENCE?

The Moose Fence trailhead is named after a tall fence installed in the 1970s to protect a research plantation of white pine from browsing moose. The fence is gone, but the moose are still here.

One skier reports that his closest encounter ever with a moose was here, on the Upland Loop. The adult moose came out of the woods and walked straight toward him. He could have touched the moose with his ski pole. ❇

Onion River Road Trailhead

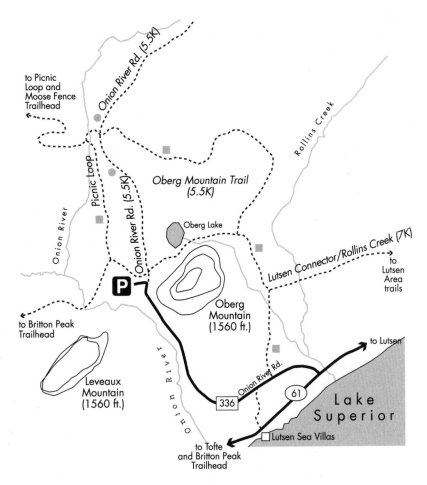

(4) Onion River Road Trailhead

Between the open views and the rolling trails, skiing this region of trails feels like skiing in the mountains.

LEVEAUX OVERLOOK (3.5K)

More difficult to most difficult. For a nice change of pace, try this in-and-out mini-adventure. After skiing 4.1K from the Leveaux trailhead along the southeastern corner of the Picnic Loop to intersection K, there's a 3K ungroomed trail that leads south to a scenic overlook (see map p. 96).

OBERG MOUNTAIN TRAIL (5.5K)

More difficult. This is a classic climb up into maple forest. Going counter-clockwise, you start with a long climb, then you'll be rewarded with a relatively long level stretch through the thick maples before a quick descent back to the Onion River Road trail. You can return to the trailhead on the Road Trail or on part of the Picnic Loop for an 8K loop. The views along the Picnic Loop are much better than the road, with Leveaux Peak rising out of open fields like a scene from the mountains of Montana.

ONION RIVER ROAD (5.5K)

Easiest. The trail is actually the continuation of Onion River Road (Forest Road 336), and is groomed nearly wide enough

SUGARBUSH TRAIL ASSOCIATION

By joining the Sugarbush Trail Association you'll help maintain, preserve and enhance the extensive Sugarbush trail system. The Association is a 501(c)(3) organization, so all donations are tax exempt. If you love these fabulously groomed trails as much as we do, you'll want to contribute to this great cause.

The Association holds meetings in the Tofte area and regularly publishes an e-mail newsletter of trail updates to members. Individual memberships are $15/year, household memberships are $25/year, and business/corporate memberships are $100/year.

See www.sugarbushtrail.org for more information and donations forms.

for side-by-side skate skiing. Late season skiers will find snow here earlier and later than other sections, sometimes skiing even into May. In poor snow years, this is the best and sometimes only groomed ski trail on the North Shore.

LUTSEN CONNECTOR/ ROLLINS CREEK (7K)

More difficult. From where they leave the Oberg Mountain Trail 1.4K from the parking lot on Onion River Road, these trails lead either 2.6K downhill to the Lutsen Sea Villas or 5K to the Superior National Golf Course. In both cases, the trails are not always groomed, so pick your way carefully.

LUTSEN TOFTE TOURISM ASSOCIATION

There are many lodging opportunities in the Lutsen-Tofte area of Highway 61. The tourism association hosts a web site rich with information about the area including resorts, attractions, maps, an events calendar, photo gallery and complete recreation guide featuring biking, canoeing/kayaking, cruises, dogsled rides, fishing, golfing, hiking, horseback riding, sightseeing and, of course, fabulous cross country skiing opportunities.

To learn about the area, visit americasnorthcoast.org

SPECTACULAR NORTH SHORE MAPLES

The sugar maple and yellow birch that cover the ridges of the Sugarbush trails are trees of the northern hardwood forest. Given its latitude, the North Shore should be too far north for this sort of forest. Yet as any fall color hiker or observant skier has noticed, sugar maples and yellow birch dominate the Sugarbush area.

Anywhere the temperature drops below about -45 F, sugar maple and yellow birch cannot survive. The North Shore ought to be a boreal forest of spruce, birch and pine, except for one important factor: the warming influence of Lake Superior. On the ridgelines where these maples grow, the warm lake keeps the temperature from dropping below that killing point, even on the coldest nights.

In the valleys of the North Shore highlands, the forest is more as it should be for this latitude. Spruce, birch and alder dominate. These valleys are frost pockets, where the cold air that sinks off the ridgeline accumulates and, cut off from the heat of the lake, reduces the temperature to ranges inhospitable to the yellow birch and sugar maple.

Broadly speaking, the ridges resemble a forest from Central Minnesota while the valleys resemble a forest in Northern Ontario. The combination of these habitats is nothing less than spectacular. ❄

Lutsen Area

Lutsen, Minnesota

24

Trailhead access

There are three trailhead locations: **(1)** Take entrance road to Superior National golf course clubhouse; **(2)** Take the Ski Hill Road (County Road 5) about 1.5 miles from Highway 61 to the stables and park by the gate; **(3)** Take Caribou Trail 1.4 miles up from Highway 61 to small parking lot on left.

Total groomed trail: 7K

Classical skiing: 7K   Skate skiing: 7K

Trail difficulty

The golf course trails can be great for beginners. The rest are basic intermediate trails.

Pass requirements

• Great Minnesota Ski Pass

Trailhead facilities

None

Snow conditions: (800) 897-7669

What makes it unique

The Superior National clubhouse is a hub for winter fun, including dog sledding, sleigh rides, and skiing on the golf course.

Information

Lutsen Tofte Tourism Association, Box 2248, Tofte MN 55615, 218) 663-7804. www.northshoreskitrail.com

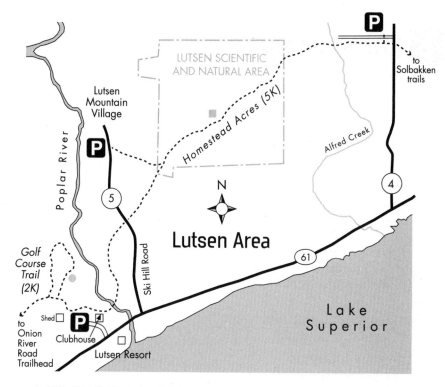

GOLF COURSE TRAIL (2K)

Easiest. This trail starts from the Superior National golf course clubhouse. Taken clockwise, it starts on the trail connecting to the Oberg/Leveaux trails and weaves in and out of fairways underneath dramatic Moose Mountain. Since much of this trail follows open golf course terrain, the track is susceptible to windblown snow. Still, it's a nice, sunny option for guests of Lutsen Resort.

HOMESTEAD ACRES (5K)

More difficult. This trail connects the Lutsen area and the Solbakken Resort trails. From the golf course trailhead, it crosses the Poplar River and County Road 36. A spur trail comes down from the Lutsen stables, where parking is available off the Ski Hill Road. The trail cuts across Trapper Pass through the Lutsen Scientific and Natural Area, with some spectacular old-growth hardwoods. Watch out for snowmobile trail crossings, as you may encounter them in the middle of a downhill run.

Lutsen Mountains Nordic Center

Lutsen, Minnesota

Trailhead access
Take Ski Hill Road (County Road 36) 2.8 miles north of Highway 61 to Lutsen Mountain. Parking is the same as for the downhill area, and you may need to take the shuttle bus from a satellite parking area.

Total groomed trail: 24K
Classical skiing: 24K   Skate skiing: 24K

Trail difficulty
Riding the chairlift with Nordic skis takes some chutzpah, but the trails themselves are also challenging, especially up on Mystery Mountain.

Pass requirements
• Day passes available at main chalet ($9/adult, $5/children).

Trailhead facilities
Full services including food and ski rental.

What makes it unique
The emphasis here is on "norpine" skiing, with chairlifts taking you to higher elevations and allowing you to ski mostly downhill.

Information
Lutsen Mountains Nordic Center, PO Box 129, Lutsen MN 55612. (218) 663-7281. www.lutsen.com.

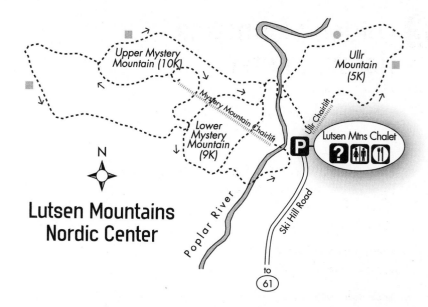

Lutsen Mountains Nordic Center

ULLR MOUNTAIN (5K)

More difficult. Take the Ullr Mountain chairlift and head straight into the woods from the top of the lift. Within moments you will leave behind the rush of the downhill slopes and enter a quiet maple forest for the first half of the downhill run. In the last 2.5K, you follow North Road overlooking the scenic Poplar River valley. Beginning skiers can just ski in from the chalet along the 2.5K of road.

MYSTERY MOUNTAIN (19K TOTAL)

More difficult. From the Ullr Mountain trail, you'll cross the Poplar River and pass an old

LUTSEN LODGING

Nordic skiers can ski right out of Caribou Highlands on to the Lutsen Area trails (see p. 104). Info at www.caribouhighlands.com.

Lodging opportunities are plenty in Lutsen. For information and reservations: www.lutsenlodgingcompany.com or www.americasnorthcoast.org

cabin in a field with a scenic view of Lutsen's Eagle Mountain. After 1K you will cross under the Mystery Mountain chair. At the next intersection, go left and continue downhill underneath the lift and across the runs of Mystery Mountain. There are some particularly sharp turns in this section, so be prepared. At the base, take the Mystery Mountain chairlift. On top you can head downhill on the trail signed #25. Another possibility is to head into the woods on trail #4 for a longer downhill run, or even take a 2K run on ungroomed trail #3.

HISTORIC LUTSEN

The town of Lutsen is named after Lützen, a village in Germany where the Swedish king Gustavus Adolphus II was killed in a 1632 battle. The only battle you will find in this Lutsen is for the best parking spaces as the North Shore's most popular winter destination rolls out its winter offerings. It wasn't nearly so crazy at the turn of the century when Carl Axel Nelson first started hosting moose hunters. That was the start of a long tradition of hospitality. Today Lutsen Mountain and Lutsen Resort provide a dynamic and far-reaching North Shore winter destination. ✳

Solbakken Resort

Lutsen, Minnesota

Trailhead access
There are two trailheads: **(1)** Park at Solbakken Resort on Highway 61, milepost 94; **(2)** Take County Road 41 (Hall Road) 0.4 miles up from Highway 61 to small lot on left.

Total groomed trail: 22.8K
Classical skiing: 22.8K   Skate skiing: 13.4K

Trail difficulty
Some of these trails are the flattest you'll find in the area. Others provide long climbs and delicious downhills.

Pass requirements
• Great Minnesota Ski Pass

Trailhead facilities
Full services at Solbakken Resort including rentals.

Snow conditions: (800) 897-7669

What makes it unique
The history of homesteading on the North Shore comes alive in these loops named after original settlers. These trails are perfect to take advantage of the ski-through system to Lutsen Area or Cascade River State Park.

Information
Solbakken Resort, 4874 W. Highway 61, Lutsen MN 55612, (218) 663-7566 or (800) 435-3950.
www.solbakkenresort.com

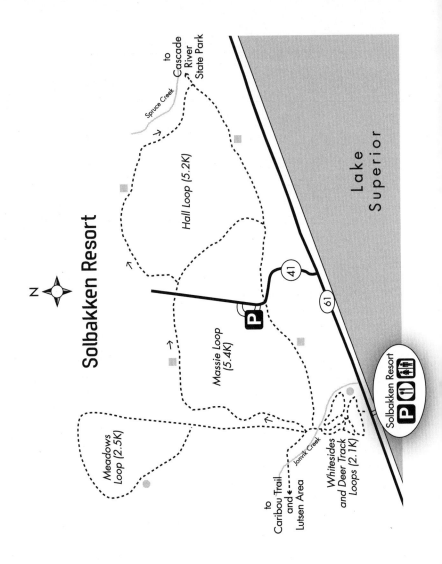

WHITESIDES/DEER TRACK LOOPS (2.1K)

Easiest and more difficult/classical and skating. The first of these two short loops is the 0.8K Deer Track Loop, named for the deer which frequent the plentiful cedar here. This is nice and flat for beginners. Whitesides Loop is a little hillier as it runs along Jonvik Creek.

CARIBOU TRAIL CONNECTOR (1.8K)

More difficult/classical and skating. This trail presents an easy opportunity for "norpine" skiing from the trailhead on the Caribou Trail about 450 vertical feet back down to Solbakken. Unlike the other trails here, this has two double tracks so you can ski side-by-side up before zooming back down again.

MEADOWS LOOP (2.5K)

Easiest/classical and skating. This loop climbs gently to the headwaters of Jonvick Creek through open terrain. Although not officially designated as a skijoring trail, you may find some skijoring action on this trail.

MASSIE LOOP (5.4K)

More difficult/partial skating. After climbing through an open area and passing the abandoned Massie homestead, enjoy a magical run through a thick grove of cedar. The upper 3K is groomed for skating.

HALL LOOP (5.2K)

More difficult/classical and skating. Continue from the top of the Massie Loop on the Hall Loop, named after the other family to homestead this area. In contrast with the Massie Loop, this is mostly evergreen trees, including scenic glades of spruce. Like the Massie Loop, the southern part of this loop is open forest, with plenty of openings for wildlife: watch for plentiful deer signs and tracks of the possible wolf that follows.

SOLBAKKEN

Solbakken Resort offers lakeshore lodging adjacent to trails. For information and reservations contact the numbers on p. 109. With Cascade Lodge, this is the heart of North Shore inn-based skiing.

SPRUCE CREEK CONNECTOR (to Cascade River State Park) (5.8K)

Easiest. The thru-skier or those who have made shuttle arrangements will enjoy this section connecting Solbakken Resort and the Cascade River State Park trails. Otherwise, it's an in-and-out option.

Cascade River State Park

Lutsen, Minnesota

Trailhead access
There are two trailheads: **(1)** Enter Cascade River State Park at milepost 100 on Highway 61 and take park road to Trail Center; **(2)** Use small parking lot at milepost 98 with access to trails on west side of river (see Cascade Lodge section, "Western Loop").

Total groomed trail: 12.5K
Classical skiing: 12.5K

Trail difficulty
Because of the variety of trails all linked together, this system is best for an intermediate skier who likes a surprise or two.

Pass requirements
• Great Minnesota Ski Pass
• Minnesota State Park vehicle permit

Trailhead facilities
Restrooms

Snow conditions: (800) 897-7669

What makes it unique
This park provides the only North Shore Mountains opportunity for Lake Superior lakeshore skiing. Trails are groomed only six feet wide, so you'll feel close to the diverse forest. The quiet little warming shack at the trailhead—or the restaurant at Cascade Lodge—lets you make a day of it on these diverse trails. With the Cascade Lodge trails and the Deer Yard trails, you've got 45K of trails to choose from right here.

Information
Cascade River State Park, 3481 W. Highway 61, Lutsen MN 55612, (218) 387-3053.
www.state.mn.us/state_parks/cascade_river

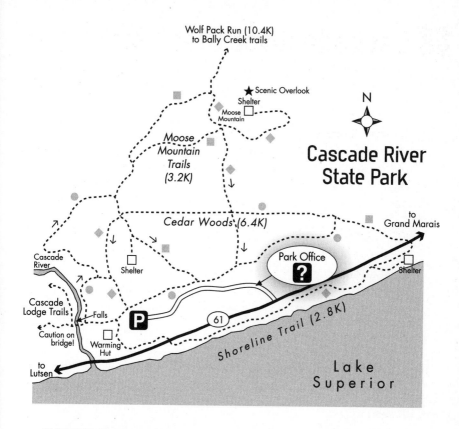

SHORELINE TRAIL (2.8K)

Easiest and more difficult. This is your only opportunity in
Cook County and the North Shore Mountains to ski right
along the shore of Lake Superior. After dropping down through
the (closed) campground and a careful crossing of Highway 61,
enjoy a challenging, twisting run a few yards from the waves or
the ice. Though signed as "Easiest," this is actually quite tricky.
Snow conditions must be optimal for good skiing on this loop.

CEDAR WOODS (6.4K)

Easiest to advanced. This is a great cruise through cedar
woods with numerous signs of deer. One-way trails force you to
plan ahead: by skiing clockwise, you can make this a beginner's
loop, starting on the river ridge trails. Otherwise, you can climb

gradually in a counterclockwise direction, then enjoy either one of two intermediate downhills or a wild advanced downhill (dropping 200 feet in 0.6K). The trails along the edge of the Cascade River Valley offer dramatic views of the valley and Lookout Mountain, set in pines.

The trail across the Cascade River is quite tricky on skis, and since you don't want to lose control close to the gorge of a rushing river, you'd be best served by taking off your skis and walking.

MOOSE MOUNTAIN TRAILS (3.2K)

Intermediate to advanced. Depart from the cedar woods and climb another 220 feet to the shelter on top of Moose Mountain. The last section of trail is a real challenge, but the view of Lake Superior is worth it.

BALLY CREEK CONNECTOR (10.4K)

See entry for Wolf Pack Run, p. 125.

TOUGH DEER ARE TOUGH ON TREES

Often the most obvious wildlife signs you will see in winter are those of the white-tailed deer. Deer develop and maintain a network of packed trails through their choice winter habitat of cedar groves. Their four stomachs allow them to browse on everything from grass to tree bark, each stomach progressively turning rough plant material into essential nutrients. Because of this browsing, the voracious deer are the single biggest obstacle to restoring native conifer forest on the North Shore.

Cascade Lodge

Lutsen, Minnesota

Trailhead access
Cascade Lodge is at Highway 61 milepost 99, ten miles southwest of Grand Marais. Reach the trailhead at the top of the road that leads through the resort, past the cabins.

Total groomed trail: 14.4K
Classical skiing: 14.4K   Skate skiing: 2.5K

Trail difficulty
Medium-wide but twisting trails make for some challenges.

Pass requirements
• Great Minnesota Ski Pass
• Other fees: $3.50/day parking for non-guests includes trail map

Trailhead facilities
Full facilities at Cascade Lodge.

Snow conditions:
(800) 897-7669

What makes it unique
Cascade Lodge provides true ski-from-your-door lodging, with access from your cabin to over 50K of Pisten-Bully groomed trail in the closely connected state park and Deer Yard systems.

Information
Cascade Lodge, 3719 W. Highway 61, Lutsen MN 55612, (218) 387-1112 or (800) 322-9543.
www.cascadelodgemn.com

CASCADE LODGE

The best trailside Nordic ski lodging right next to Lake Superior is found here, including cabins and lodge rooms. Meals and trail lunches are available at the restaurant next door. For information and reservations, contact Cascade Lodge at the numbers listed on this page.

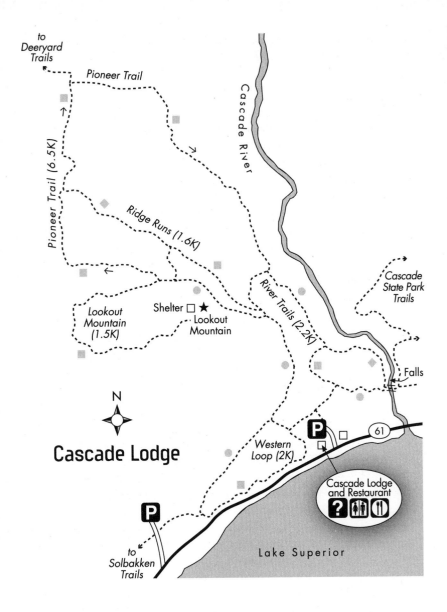

RIVER TRAILS (2.2K)

Easiest to advanced/classical only. These are classic, old-fashioned ski trails with tight turns and abrupt, sometimes steep hills. These trails are used extensively by hikers and snowshoers in winter (the Superior Hiking Trail shares the trail), so use caution and snowplowing skills. Nice views of the Cascade River gorge.

PIONEER TRAIL (6.5K)

Intermediate/skating and classical. This is the primary large loop of the Cascade Lodge system. The first 1.5K are on a wide roadbed, groomed for skating and are rated easiest. After the junction with the Lookout Mountain trail, the trail narrows and gets more difficult, with a long herringbone climb right at the start. The trail continues with level terrain interspersed with short climbs, past the junction with Upper Ridge Run up to 1,250 feet before descending back into the state park and to the lodge.

UPPER AND LOWER RIDGE RUNS (1.6K)

Intermediate to advanced/classical only. These are literally runs down a ridge, cutting off from the Pioneer Loop. As you approach the last leg of the Upper Ridge Run, have a good snowplow ready as you will be zooming nonstop through a twisting tunnel of balsam fir. There is also a challenging hill midway down the Lower Ridge Run.

LOOKOUT MOUNTAIN (1.5K)

Intermediate/classical only. Take your time on an almost 500-foot climb to the top. The trail narrows and steepens after leaving the Pioneer Trail. After the bulk of the climb, where you will have to herringbone a few times, the trail narrows and then shares space with the Superior Hiking Trail for a twisting run along the ridge top. There is a shelter on top to rest up before the glide down. The view is nice although obscured by birch trees unless you scamper below the shelter.

WESTERN LOOP (2.0K)

Easiest/classical and skating. This loop has multiple personalities. On the northern half you are on a wide road with virtually no curves. On the southern half, you are in dark woods, with significant hills and turns. Although marked "easy," this southern half is definitely trickier than the northern, so be careful with beginners. From the western end of the loop, it's a skate-able 0.4K to a small state park parking lot, and then much farther on to the Solbakken Resort and Lutsen Area trails.

SOLBAKKEN CONNECTOR

See Spruce Creek Connector, p. 111.

SKIING NORTH SHORE RIVERS

The North Shore in winter offers a select few experiences that push the boundaries of common sense and, in return, offer extraordinary rewards. There aren't major mountains to conquer, and even the foolish stay off of Lake Superior in the winter. But skiing a North Shore river is a peak experience.

In winter, the rivers of the North Shore are snowy paths through an apparent wilderness. Travel a river farther up from the highway and you are almost guaranteed seclusion. You will get no grand, sweeping views, but rather an intimate sense of the deep winter environment. Signs of animals are everywhere.

January and February are the best months for river travel, since they provide the coldest temperatures and the deepest snow. If you've never skied a river before, go with someone who has.

For first-time river skiers:
- Sucker River
- Knife River
- Kadunce River

For intermediate river skiers:
- Amity Creek and Lester River
- Gooseberry River, above Fifth Falls
- Split Rock River ✳

Deer Yard

Lutsen, Minnesota

Trailhead access

From Highway 61, take County Road 7 (Pike Lake Road)
either from Grand Marais or from Milepost 101 to County
Road 45, then continue 4.1 miles west on 45 past intersection
of County Roads 44 and 45. At the intersection of Pike Lake
Road, Murmur Road and a logging road, take Murmur Road
(Forest Road #332) 0.7 miles to trailhead, a small parking area
off a turn in the road.

Total groomed trail: 18K

Classical skiing: 18K

Trail difficulty

There are no short loops here, so even the intermediate trails
become a logistical challenge to prepare for.

Pass requirements

• Great Minnesota Ski Pass

Trailhead facilities

None

Snow conditions: (800) 897-7669

What makes it unique

This area is remote and yet very well-maintained, with Cascade
Lodge groomers coming all the way up from the shore. The
variety of landscape and scenery makes for a nice all-day outing.

Information

Cascade Lodge, 3719 W. Highway 61, Lutsen MN 55612,
(218) 387-1112 or (800) 322-9543.
www.cascadelodgemn.com

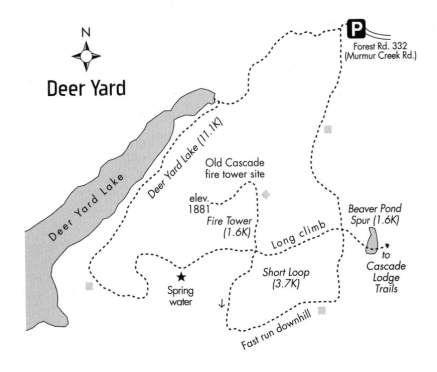

DEER YARD LAKE (11.1K)

Intermediate. This is a wonderful half-day trip around a high ridge and along the cedar-lined shore of Deer Yard Lake. The truly ambitious can include this loop as part of a full-day ski up from Cascade River State Park. Traveling counterclockwise, you will experience a variety of forests. Glide down into the old cedars of Deer Yard Lake, and enjoy a break on the lake at its eastern end where a rough trail leads down onto the shore. Stop for spring water in the middle of a typical North Shore maple and yellow-birch forest. A long hill takes you by the first trail intersection you've seen in 7K. In the last stretch, conifers hold close to the trail.

FIRE TOWER (1.6K)

Advanced. Climb an additional 200 feet to the former site of a fire tower from which there is a good view of Deer Yard Lake. Trail is marked by blue arrows.

SHORT LOOP (3.7K)

More difficult to advanced. Break up your climb on the long loop or, if you are not doing the long loop, take this trail on your way back to the trailhead.

BEAVER POND SPUR (1.6K)

More difficult. A short run along the trail takes you to a wide-open beaver meadows, a nice contrast from the relatively dense forest of the Deer Yard Loop. This trail connects Deer Yard with the rest of the Cascade system.

OH, THE BIRDS YOU'LL SEE!

There are over 80 birds known to live in this area year-round.

Common birds you are likely to see on a full-day winter outing:
- Black-capped chickadee
- Raven
- Ruffed grouse
- Downy woodpecker
- Red-breasted nuthatch

Birds less frequently seen:
- Pine grosbeak
- Blue jay
- Gray jay
- Bald eagle
- Hairy woodpecker
- Owls, including Barred, Boreal and Saw-whet

Invasive, flocking birds:
- Common redpoll
- Pine siskin
- Bohemian waxwing
- Crossbill ✳

Downy woodpecker

Bally Creek

Grand Marais, Minnesota

Trailhead access
From Highway 61, take Cook County Road 7 about 4 miles to County Road 48, which joins Forest Road 158. Take 158 for 2.1 miles to end.

Total groomed trail: 30.4K
Classical skiing: 30.4K   Skate skiing: 8K

Trail difficulty
Most of these trails are narrower, more winding "traditional" ski trails.

Pass requirements
• Great Minnesota Ski Pass

Trailhead facilities
None. Cabin rental and lodging information at www.bear-track.com

Snow conditions: (800) 897-7669

What makes it unique
Rustic cabins allow overnight experiences. Although connected to the North Shore Mountains system, this section preserves a traditional skiing atmosphere with narrow trails groomed by snowmobile.

Information
Bear Track Outfitting Co., Box 937, Grand Marais MN 55604, (218) 387-1162 or (800) 795-8068.
www.bear-track.com

Bally Creek

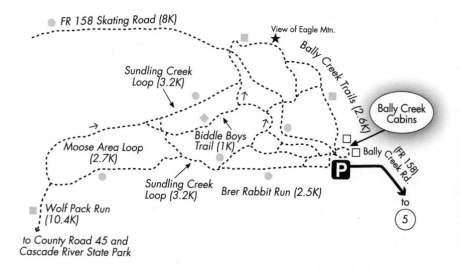

FR 158 Skating Road (8K)

View of Eagle Mtn.

Bally Creek Trails (2.6K)

Sundling Creek Loop (3.2K)

Bally Creek Cabins

Moose Area Loop (2.7K)

Biddle Boys Trail (1K)

Bally Creek Rd. (FR 158)

Sundling Creek Loop (3.2K)

Brer Rabbit Run (2.5K)

P

Wolf Pack Run (10.4K)

to 5

to County Road 45 and Cascade River State Park

BRER RABBIT RUN (2.5K)

Easier/classical only. This tight network of trails is perfect for a wandering warm-up when you don't want to think hard but would rather focus on skiing. The nice coniferous woods invite you to poke around.

SUNDLING CREEK LOOP (3.2K)

Easier/classical only. This trail wanders through the woods with tight but easygoing turns. The forest is mostly mixed birch, spruce and fir. The trail loops around the "wildlife ponds," a large marshy area. On the north side of the loop the trail follows a Forest Service road, so it widens and flattens out before the last stretch back to the trailhead.

BIDDLE BOYS TRAIL (1.0K)

Advanced/classical only. This trail is the exception to the generally level and easy terrain of the Bally Creek trails. It rolls up and down and up and down through piney woods. It's a fun and tiring way to end a longer, easier loop.

MOOSE AREA LOOP (2.7K)

Easier/classical only. This loop adds both distance and variety of habitat to the Sundling Creek Loop. The southern side of the loop is largely in clearings favored by moose, while the northern side of the loop (after the "Big Cedar Tree" which marks the junction with the connector trail to Cascade State Park) is largely pine plantation, with jack and red pine. This section is known locally as "Bullwinkle Run."

BALLY CREEK CAMP

These wood-heated, rustic cabins are located right within the Bally Creek trail system. Pets are welcome; a separate trail is available for skijoring. Information and reservations: Bear Track Outfitting Co., (218) 387-1162 or (800) 795-8068. www.bear-track.com/cabins

BALLY CREEK TRAILS (2.6K)

Intermediate/classical only. Though marked as easy, these are tricky trails, with steep, narrow downhills. Numerous cleared areas add to the variety and the views. The trails climb to elevations of over 1740 feet, easily some of the highest terrain in the whole North Shore skiing system, with a distant view to Eagle Mountain, the highest point in Minnesota (it's the peak on the right).

SKATING ROAD (8K)

Easy/classical and skating. This is the continuation of the same road you came in on, unplowed. As a wide and flat Forest Service road, it's perfect for skate skiing. It's also tracked for classical skiing, so bring your first-timers here and ski alongside them.

WOLF PACK RUN (CASCADE CONNECTOR) (10.4K)

Intermediate/classical only. Only the aerobically crazy will choose to ski this trail uphill, with its 900 feet elevation gain from Cascade River State Park. Instead, get a buddy or an innkeeper to deliver you to the Bally Creek trailhead, ski through the system and enjoy the nearly 1,000-foot drop over 14K or more of trail. The connector takes you through moose and wolf country with beautiful views of Lake Superior. You can cut this in half by just doing the bottom half from County Road 45.

DISCOVERING A WOLF KILL

As you zoom along a ski trail, an odd feeling shakes you particularly alert to your surroundings. At first, you notice a tuft of brown or white fur loose in the breeze...and maybe an odd combination of critter tracks, like deer and raven. Perhaps there is a grove of cedar trees ahead. You feel a tingle run up your spine; the hair on the back of your neck bristles. Then, not just a tuft of brown fur is visible but a clump of skin, too. The groomed ski track is trampled under a chaos of animal trails: comb-marks from the wing tips of food-laden ravens taking off, and wolf scat, fresh enough so that it's still brown and moist. Just off the trail in the cedars, you see what's left of a white-tailed deer. You hear the ravens in the trees, squawking. You know the wolves crouch somewhere, watching as you gingerly ski around their prey. The scene marks the end of one life as well as the continuance of many others. ❄

Gunflint Trail

Take a short drive up and away from the North Shore to skiers' heaven. This is the wild Boundary Waters, complete with remote lakes, fresh forest fires and blowdowns. The resorts of the Gunflint Trail have assembled a pure skiing experience, from their dueling Pisten-Bully groomers to their saunas, heated trail shelters and wax rooms. Whether you are circling the lakes in the Central Gunflint, climbing the ridges of the Upper Gunflint, or curving around Pincushion Mountain, you will be immersed in skiing and skiing only. Take a trip down the Banadad Trail, staying in a yurt halfway along, and you will complete the Gunflint experience.

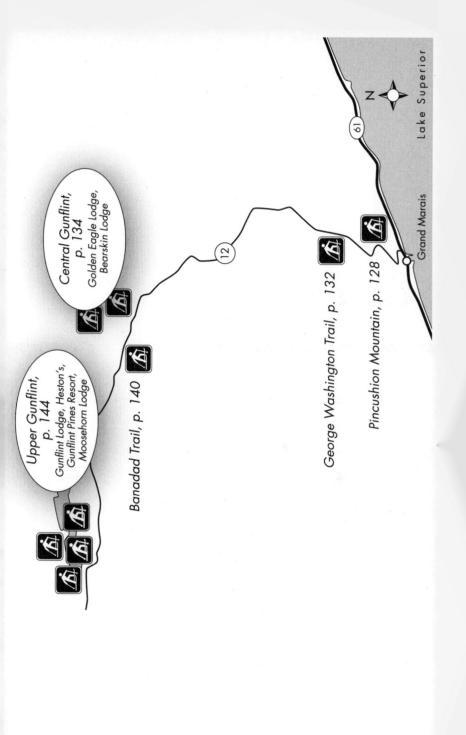

Central Gunflint, p. 134
Golden Eagle Lodge,
Bearskin Lodge

Upper Gunflint,
p. 144
Gunflint Lodge, Heston's,
Gunflint Pines Resort,
Moosehorn Lodge

Banadad Trail, p. 140

George Washington Trail, p. 132

Pincushion Mountain, p. 128

61

12

N

Lake Superior

Grand Marais

Pincushion Mountain

Grand Marais, Minnesota

Trailhead access
Take Gunflint Trail 1.7 miles north from Highway 61 in Grand Marais and enter the Pincushion trailhead road on right. Registered guests only can enter from Pincushion Bed & Breakfast road a little farther up the Gunflint Trail.

Total groomed trail: 23K
Classical skiing: 23K   Skate skiing: 23K

Trail difficulty
Consistent grooming and wide trails make this system accessible for all levels, although longer loops and steeper hills are better for more advanced skiers.

Pass requirements
- Great Minnesota Ski Pass
- Recommended donation of $5/person/day to support the North Superior Ski and Run Club, which administers this trail system. A yellow donation box is located on the main entrance sign, just below the warming chalet.

Trailhead facilities
Outhouse, warming chalet at public trailhead.

Snow conditions: (800) 897-7669 or www.gunflint-trail.com

What makes it unique
These are some of the only trails on the shore designed by skiers specifically for skiers, and it shows. The trails have a real community feel, from the tourists sharing the fabulous parking lot view to the sign that lists the Grand Marais businesses that support the Club.

Information
North Superior Ski and Run Club, PO Box 542, Grand Marais MN 55604. 218-387-3373. www.pincushiontrails.org

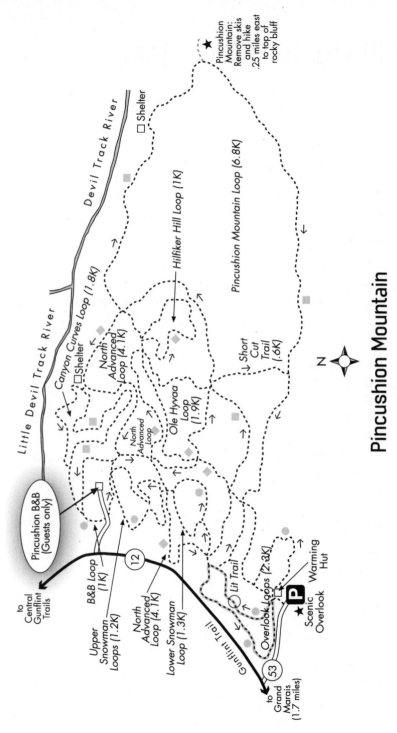

Pincushion Mountain: Remove skis and hike .25 miles east to top of rocky bluff

□ Shelter

Devil Track River

Little Devil Track River

Canyon Curves Loop (1.8K)

□ Shelter

North Advanced Loop (4.1K)

Hilfiker Hill Loop (1K)

Pincushion Mountain Loop (6.8K)

Short Cut Trail (.6K)

North Advanced Loop

Ole Hyvaa Loop (1.9K)

Pincushion B&B (Guests only)

to Central Gunflint Trails

B&B Loop (1K)

Upper Snowman Loops (1.2K)

12

North Advanced Loop (4.1K)

Lower Snowman Loop (1.3K)

Gunflint Trail

Lit Trail

Overlook Loops (2.3K)

Warming Hut

P

Scenic Overlook

53

to Grand Marais (1.7 miles)

N

Pincushion Mountain

OVERLOOK LOOPS (2.3K)

Easier/partly lighted. These two loops start and end at the public trailhead and are named for their location near this overlook rather than any view from the trails themselves. The West Overlook Loop (1.3K) is lighted at night; a steady climb starts it off. The East Overlook Loop, at 1K, is separated from the rest of the traffic but is a little hillier than the west loop, making it less suited for real beginners.

PINCUSHION MOUNTAIN LOOP (6.8K)

Intermediate. Follow the signs through the first four intersections as you head out on this loop. Although rated intermediate, this trail offers relatively easy skiing and provides a nice morning or afternoon outing through a mature birch forest. Much of the section over the river is also the Superior Hiking Trail. Stretch out the day by snacking at the shelter overlooking the Devil Track River valley and taking off your skis to walk 0.25 mile to the top of Pincushion Mountain itself for a wide view of Lake Superior.

PINCUSHION BED & BREAKFAST

Pincushion B&B was built and is managed by skiers for skiers and is located on a forested ridge overlooking Lake Superior. Hiking, mountain biking, and cross country ski trails connect to the B&B. Four cozy guest rooms are available. Information and reservations: 968 Gunflint Trail, Grand Marais MN 55604, (218) 387-1276 or (800) 542-1226. www.pincushionbb.com

NORTH ADVANCED LOOP (4.1K)

Advanced. This loop is carved out of the hilly central section of the trail system; once again, the clear signs allow you to skip reading maps and just follow the arrows. Ski this loop a couple of times and watch for the transition into and out of a nearly pure birch forest from a mixture of aspen, spruce and fir.

LOWER AND UPPER SNOWMAN (2.5K)

Easier. Carved into the existing trail network in 2004, these three loops are stacked on top of each other like, well, a snowman. Although surrounded by advanced trails, these are easy open loops.

B&B LOOP (1K)

Easier. This trail is perfect for guests of Pincushion B&B to try out their skills before heading out on the advanced trails.

CANYON CURVES LOOP (1.8K)

Intermediate. This trail lives up to its name right away as you descend from the B&B Loop down a curvy trail. The trail loops and turns through birch and fir before a final run along the rim of the Little Devil Track River. Take a second loop around before you grunt back up the hill.

OLE HYVAA AND HILFIKER HILL LOOPS (2.9K)

Advanced. These are rolling trails in the tradition of adventurous Nordic skiing, as seen in their names. The 1.9K Ole Hyvaa Loop is loosely translated from the Finnish for "Oh my God!" The 1K Hilfiker Hill Loop is named after Dr. Hilfiker, an early ski enthusiast who lived near the trails in the early 1970s. Parts of these loops may be shared with the Superior Hiking Trail.

NEVER A BAD DAY IN GRAND MARAIS

It's raining in February, the result of an unusual warm spell. Or it's 10 below zero and the wind is howling. You could go skiing, but something says you're not that crazy. Instead, head into town and enjoy some North Shore culture.

Cruise the aisles of Joynes Ben Franklin Department Store for woolen wear, toys for the kids, or comfy shoes. Check out regional art at Sivertson Gallery or the Johnson Heritage Post. Sip a microbrew at the Gunflint Tavern. Enjoy a Blizzard at DQ. A day in Grand Marais without skiing is not so bad, after all. ✿

George Washington Trail

Grand Marais, Minnesota

Trailhead access
Take Gunflint Trail 7 miles north from Highway 61 in Grand Marais to parking lot on left.

Total trail: 3.5K
Groomed once a week, this trail is open to all uses including snowshoe and dog walking.

Trail difficulty
Easy skiing on level trails, but watch out for dog and people tracks.

Pass requirements
• None

Trailhead facilities
None

What makes it unique
This gentle little loop provides a quiet alternative to the large trail systems typical of the Gunflint region. This pine plantation was planted in 1932 by Boy Scouts from Grand Marais to reforest an area hard hit by logging and fires.

Information
Superior National Forest, Gunflint Ranger District, 2020 W. Highway 61, Grand Marais, MN 55604 (218) 387-1750. gunflint@fs.fed.us

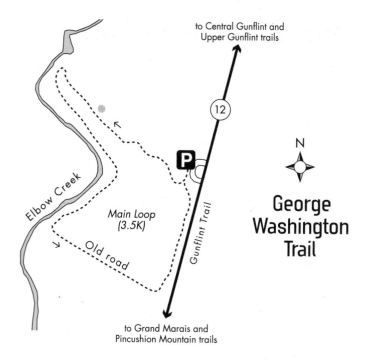

to Central Gunflint and
Upper Gunflint trails

12

N

Elbow Creek

P

Main Loop
(3.5K)

Old road

Gunflint Trail

George
Washington
Trail

to Grand Marais and
Pincushion Mountain trails

MAIN LOOP (3.5K)

Easier. Although groomed only occasionally, this simple loop is
used often enough by both local skiers and respectful snowshoers
that you can generally count on a decent trail. The counterclockwise loop starts and ends in the pine plantation for which
it is named, but along the way there is a wide variety of forest
types, as well as mellow little Elbow Creek.

PEACEFUL COEXISTENCE IN THE WOODS

George Washington himself might have been proud. Is this trail
for skiers or for dog walkers? Or for both? Let the people vote!
Good ski grooming does not go with dog walking. Yet people
love to get out in the woods with their dogs. Conflict between
users led to proposals to either ban dogs or stop volunteer
grooming here. After an informal vote in 2005, the trail remains
open to all non-motorized users. ✿

⛷ Central Gunflint

Grand Marais, Minnesota

33

Trailhead access
Take the Gunflint Trail north from Grand Marais to either:
(1) Bearskin Lodge: Drive 26 miles on the Gunflint Trail, take right at Bearskin Lodge sign, continue short distance to Lodge office; or **(2) Golden Eagle Lodge:** Drive 28 miles on the Gunflint Trail, take right on Clearwater Road, continue for 3.5 miles to Lodge office.

Total groomed trail: 55K
Classical skiing: 55K   Skate skiing: 34K   Lighted trail: 2.1K

Trail difficulty
A bit of everything, from flat wide beginner trails to steep and twisty expert terrain.

Pass requirements
• Jointly managed by Bearskin and Golden Eagle Lodges. Free for guests of lodges. For others, day passes ($12/day) and season passes are available at trailheads.

Trailhead facilities
Full facilities at both trailheads, including snacks and ski rental. Trail maps given when purchasing tickets at trailhead offices.

Snow conditions: (800) 897-7669 or www.gunflint-trail.com. Trail webcam at www.golden-eagle.com

What makes it unique
Two lodges cooperate here to maintain an excellent and vast network of trails ideally suited for a family cross country ski vacation. Half of the trails are considered intermediate.

Information
Golden Eagle Lodge or Bearskin Lodge (see contact info on next page).

Bearskin Lodge Area Trails

SUMMER HOME ROAD/CAMPGROUND (5K)

Easier/classical and skating/partially lighted. This is a central corridor for Bearskin Lodge area trails, and because it is built on roads, it can be groomed more aggressively than other sections. When conditions are marginal everywhere else in northern Minnesota, this may be the only decent skiing you will find. It is wide and mostly level, good for families and beginners. The 1999 blowdown is quite obvious on the eastern end of this trail. A combination of parts of the Beaver Dam Trail, Summer Home Road and North-South Link form a 1.5K loop lighted at night by a string of Christmas lights.

OX CART TRAIL (4K)

Easier to Intermediate/classical only. This "lollipop loop" is mostly easy, intimate skiing. Since it's groomed only for classical stride, classical skiers can enjoy the quiet woods at their own pace. After crossing a beaver pond, the trail climbs gently into pine woods. Take the whole loop back to the lodge and you've skied 5.2K.

BEAR CUB WORLD CUP (8K)

Advanced/classical and skating. If you want a wild ride and are ready to push

CENTRAL GUNFLINT LODGING

Bearskin Lodge and Golden Eagle Lodge both offer excellent accommodations for skiers and direct access to the trails they jointly manage.

Bearskin Lodge
Gunflint Trail, 124 E. Bearskin Road, Grand Marais MN 55604, (218) 388-2292 or (800) 338-4170. www.bearskin.com

Golden Eagle Lodge
Cozy cabins line the shore of Flour Lake, with ski trails interlaced for true ski-from-the-door convenience. Info: Gunflint Trail, 468 Clearwater Road, Grand Marais MN 55604, (218) 388-2203 or (800) 346-2203. www.golden-eagle.com

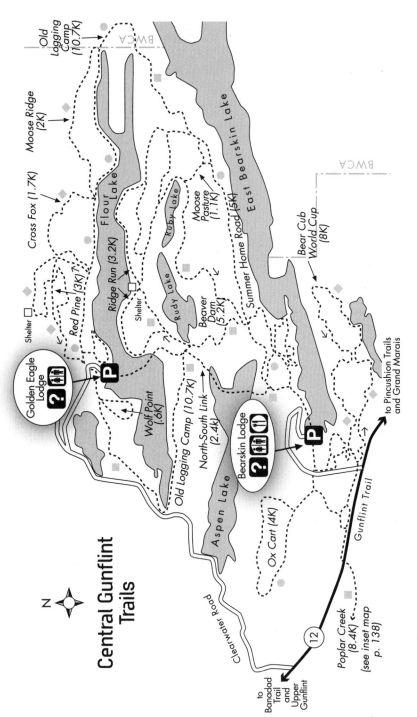

Central Gunflint Trails

N

Old Logging Camp (10.7K)

BWCA

Moose Ridge (2K)

Cross Fox (1.7K)

Flour Lake

East Bearskin Lake

Red Pine (3K)

Ridge Run (3.2K)

Ruby Lake

Rudy Lake

Moose Pasture (1.1K)

Summer Home Road (5K)

BWCA

Beaver Dam (5.2K)

Bear Cub World Cup (8K)

Shelter

Shelter

Golden Eagle Lodge

? 🛏️⬅️

P

Wolf Point (.6K)

Old Logging Camp (10.7K)

North-South Link (2.4K)

Bearskin Lodge

? 🛏️🍴

P

to Pincushion Trails and Grand Marais

Aspen Lake

Ox Cart (4K)

Gunflint Trail

Clearwater Road

12

Poplar Creek (8.4K) (see inset map p. 138)

to Banadad Trail and Upper Gunflint

for it, this is the trail to test your abilities. Think Lycra and wild aerodynamic sunglasses. The trail was designed specifically for challenging skate skiing, including steep uphills and "screaming" downhills.

POPLAR CREEK (8.4K)

Easier to Intermediate/classical only. This loop (see map p. 138) makes for a round trip of 10.2K from the junction with the Oxcart Trail. The loop takes you away from the main network of trails, across the Gunflint Trail into a quiet country of small lakes, bogs and meandering streams. A shelter halfway around makes a nice break on a day-long outing. The northern part of this section is also the beginning of the Banadad Trail (see p. 140).

NORTH-SOUTH LINK (2.4K)

Advanced/classical and skating. Although half of this trail is on the flat surface of lakes, it earns an advanced rating partially because of some steep hills and partially because of the potential hazards of lake skiing. Stay on the groomed trails and, if in doubt, ask at one of the lodges before heading out.

Golden Eagle Lodge Area Trails

OLD LOGGING CAMP (10.7K)

Easiest to advanced/classical and skating. This is the main part of a 13–14K loop around Flour Lake. East of Golden Eagle Lodge the trail follows an old logging railroad leading to the site of a historic logging camp, complete with "timber jays." After a brief and hilly passage over the boundary of the BWCA, the trail disappears into the Bearskin-area trail network. The trail reemerges on the west end of Rudy Lake for a wild ride on top of glacial eskers around the end of Flour Lake. You can cut this loop in half with the North-South Link.

WOLF POINT (0.6K)

Intermediate/classical only/lighted. This is Golden Eagle Lodge's night skiing loop, lighted by small white electric lights. The hills that are fun by day are thrilling at night.

N

Central Gunflint Trails: Poplar Creek

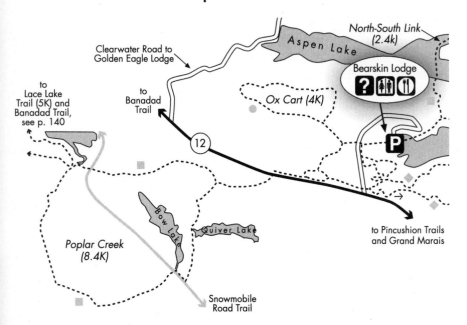

North-South Link (2.4k)

Aspen Lake

Clearwater Road to Golden Eagle Lodge

Bearskin Lodge

to Lace Lake Trail (5K) and Banadad Trail, see p. 140

to Banadad Trail

Ox Cart (4K)

12

Bow Lake

Quiver Lake

Poplar Creek (8.4K)

to Pincushion Trails and Grand Marais

Snowmobile Road Trail

NORTH FLOUR LOOPS (6.7K)

Advanced/classical and skating. Three side trails roll off an easy section of the Old Logging Camp Trail. Each trail climbs through blowdown to ridges with views both south over the lakes and north into Canada. The Red Pine loops total 3K, lead through blowdown and a young red pine forest and have a shelter on top with a view of West Bearskin Lake. The Cross Fox Trail has 1.7K of up and down. Finally, Moose Ridge offers a steep climb to Canadian views and a roller coaster ride back down to Old Logging Camp Trail.

MOOSE PASTURE (1.1K)

Easier/classical and skating. These open woods are the result of forest management as well as the 1999 blowdown and provide good winter habitat for moose. You may be visited by gray jays here; bring some extra snacks just in case.

RIDGE RUN TRAIL (6K)

Intermediate to advanced/classical only. This new trail runs along the ridge overlooking Flour Lake. Watch for sharp turns and great views. The overlooks on Flour Lake are dramatic and could make you say, "It looks just like the Boundary Waters!"

BEAVER DAM TRAIL (5.2K)

Easier to intermediate/classical only. Loop clockwise around Rudy and Ruby Lakes on this varied trail. There are some wild downhills along the southern part of the loop. You can really see the varied effects of the blowdown here. There is a shelter halfway around, overlooking Flour Lake.

THE 4TH OF JULY BLOWDOWN, 1999

In 20 minutes, powerful forces claimed centuries of old-growth forest and set the stage for decades of recovery. Straight-line winds of up to 100 miles per hour flattened almost 500,000 acres of forest from Ely to the Gunflint Trail. What had been deep, intimate forests before the storm became first tangled webs of tree trunks, then open areas as many trees were logged.

The visual impact on Gunflint ski trails was dramatic. Over half of the trails lead through blowdown areas. Nearly ten years later, new growth is coming up and the skiing is as great as ever. But the evidence of the big blow will last for decades to come.

❀

Banadad Trail
Grand Marais, Minnesota

34

Trailhead access
The main access is at the Poplar Creek Guesthouse B&B, two miles off the Gunflint Trail on the Lima Grade (Forest Road 315) and the Little Ollie Road. At the western end, there is some parking at Rib Lake Road, 0.25 mile southeast of Loon Lake Public Landing.

Total groomed trail: 34.8K
Classical skiing: 34.8K

Trail difficulty
The Banadad is generally a level, easy trail, but because it heads through remote wilderness areas, is best for experienced skiers only.

Pass requirements
- Great Minnesota Ski Pass
- BWCA Wilderness day-use permit (available at wilderness boundary or through outfitters).

Trailhead facilities
Parking for day-use is available at the Poplar Creek Guesthouse B&B, $10 per car.

Snow conditions: (800) 897-7669 or www.gunflint-trail.com

What makes it unique
This is the region's premiere wilderness trail experience, providing a wonderful combination of groomed trails and deep wilderness, plus unusual accommodation in yurts complete with Mongolian dinners.

Information
Boundary Country Trekking, 7925 Gunflint Trail, Grand Marais MN 55604, (218) 388-9972 or (800) 322-8327.
www.boundarycountry.com

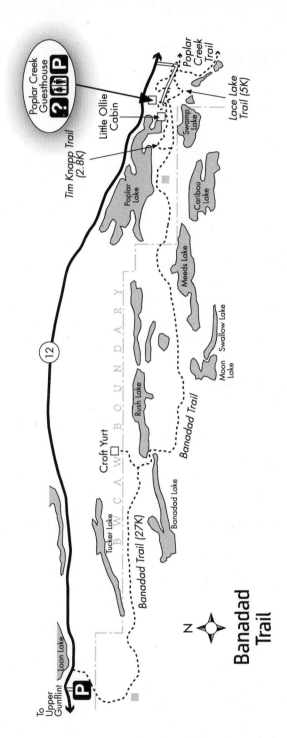

Poplar Creek Guesthouse

? 🏠 P

Little Ollie Cabin

Tim Knapp Trail (2.8K)

Poplar Creek Trail

Lace Lake Trail (5K)

Swamp Lake

Poplar Lake

Caribou Lake

Meeds Lake

Swallow Lake

Moon Lake

12

Banadad Trail

Rush Lake

Croft Yurt

B W C A W   B O U N D A R Y

Banadad Lake

Banadad Trail (27K)

Tucker Lake

Loon Lake

To Upper Gunflint

P

N

Banadad Trail

BANADAD TRAIL (27K)

Here it is, the ultimate combination of groomed trail and wilderness skiing. The Banadad Trail is 27K of nearly pure wilderness experience. Most skiers will want or need to break up the trip by staying overnight either in a yurt or a cabin operated by Boundary Country Trekking. They say that "Banadad" means "lost" in Anishinabe, but don't worry: the trail is well-marked and well-groomed.

The trail is all on land, not on lakes, so slush is not a factor. For a few miles in the middle, the trail follows the Laurentian Divide, which separates the Lake Superior watershed from the Hudson Bay watershed. In the western end, look for beaver ponds, while throughout the trail you will find open spruce bogs and dense forest. Cliffs parallel the trail at times.

The trail was created in the early 1980s out of logging roads left over from before 1978, the year logging was banned in the BWCA. The old roadbed provides a smooth skiing surface, and remnants of old logging camps give you history to ponder. Before the major national long-distance ski races became dominated by skaters, the Banadad was often used as training for races such as the Birkebeiner. But no one should race through this wonderful country anymore. Take your time and enjoy a backcountry classic.

BANADAD TRAIL LODGING

Complete your Banadad Trail experience by staying overnight in a yurt or trailside cabin. Spend your first night at the eastern end, at Tall Pines Yurt, Little Ollie cabin or in the Poplar Creek Guesthouse. Then head west on the trail to the Croft yurt, where your bags and a hot supper await you. The last day, your car will be waiting for you at the western end of the trail.

For more information, visit Boundary Country Trekking at www. boundarycountry.com or call 800-322-8327

You can arrange the all-important shuttle through Poplar Creek Guesthouse B&B or with other lodges.

TIM KNAPP TRAIL (2.8K)

Easier. This trail is well suited for those guests staying at the Poplar Creek Guesthouse B&B or Little Ollie Cabin. The Tim Knapp Trail was named for a University of Minnesota professor and skier vital to the renaissance of skiing.

LACE LAKE (5K)

Easier to intermediate. The casual visitor to Banadad country may ski this loop as part of a long day's outing from Bearskin Lodge off the Poplar Creek Trail, but to get the full flavor visit Ted and Barb Young at Poplar Creek Guesthouse B&B. This loop takes you right up to the edge of the BWCA and along scenic Poplar Creek.

THE HAM LAKE FIRE, SPRING 2007

In these woods, the only constant is change. A massive forest fire was burning around the upper Gunflint Trail as this book went to press. Severe drought conditions plus potential fuel from the 1999 blowdown storm made for dangerous fire conditions in May 2007.

The human-caused fire started near a campsite at Ham Lake, right by the Ham Lake ski trail. After burning north past Seagull Lake, the fire burned near the Magnetic Rock Trail, crossed into Canada, and looped around the north shore of Gunflint Lake. Then, a tongue of the fire ran back along the eastern side of Gunflint Lake and Loon Lake, crossed the Gunflint Trail, and burned near Rush Lake and the middle of the Banadad Trail. Over 74,000 acres were burned in the U.S. and Canada.

The upper Gunflint Trail was evacuated and the fire destroyed over 100 buildings. Fortunately, no lives were lost and the lodges reopened. Skiing on the Gunflint Trail remains excellent, and when you ski on these trails, you'll be witnessing ecological history. ❁

Upper Gunflint

Grand Marais, Minnesota

Trailhead access
Take the Gunflint Trail to the Upper Gunflint lodges (see map). Once you have a pass, you can start at Loon Lake Boat Access or the Scenic Overlook on the Gunflint Trail, in addition to the lodges.

Total groomed trail: 66.5K
Classical skiing: 66.5K   Skate skiing: 17.4K

Trail difficulty
Not much for a real beginner here, but lots of challenging terrain for the experienced skier.

Pass requirements
• Passes available at all resorts ($5/day, $10/three days or $25/week). Price includes trail map.

Trailhead facilities
Full facilities at resort trailheads. Rental available at Gunflint Lodge. All skiers should check in and buy their passes at the resorts.

Snow conditions: (800) 897-7669 or www.gunflint-trail.com

What makes it unique
Like the Central Gunflint system, the Upper Gunflint system is an amazing skiing resource, with ski-from-your-door convenience and an incredible variety of terrain. These trails are better for experienced skiers, since there are few real beginner trails near the lodges.

Information
See lodge listings on p. 148.

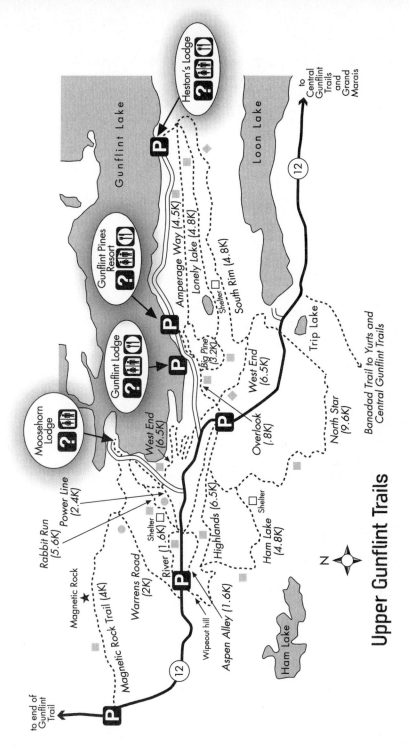

Heston's Lodge

Gunflint Pines Resort

Gunflint Lodge

Moosehorn Lodge

Gunflint Lake

Loon Lake

to Central Gunflint Trails and Grand Marais

12

Amperage Way (4.5K)

Lonely Lake (4.8K)

Shelter

South Rim (4.8K)

Big Pine (3.2K)

West End (6.5K)

Trip Lake

West End (6.5K)

Overlook (.8K)

North Star (9.6K)

Banadad Trail to Yurts and Central Gunflint Trails

Rabbit Run (5.6K)

Power Line (2.4K)

Magnetic Rock Trail (4K)

Magnetic Rock

Warrens Road (2K)

River (1.6K)

Shelter

Highlands (6.5K)

Shelter

Ham Lake (4.8K)

Wipeout hill

Aspen Alley (1.6K)

Ham Lake

N

to end of Gunflint Trail

12

Upper Gunflint Trails

Northwest trails, accessed from Moosehorn Lodge or Warrens Road parking area

POWER LINE (2.4K)

Easiest/classical only. This double-tracked trail provides access to the trails for guests of Moosehorn Lodge and vacation homes along County Road 46 (unfortunately, from Moosehorn you have to use the road to cross a Gunflint Lake bay) and makes for an accessible loop through Aspen Alley, Warrens Road and the Cut Across Trail.

WARRENS ROAD (2K)/CUT ACROSS TRAIL (1.6K)

Easier to intermediate/classical only. Warrens Road is an easy and fast double-tracked trail from a gravel pit to a three-way intersection with the Magnetic Rock Trail. The Cut Across Trail is rated more difficult, but the cautious beginner should have no problem (and should have some fun) on these gradual hills.

MAGNETIC ROCK (4K)

Intermediate to advanced/classical only. From the intersection with the Cut Across Trail, this remote trail leads past a small pond, a fire burn and a 60-foot high glacial erratic that will make your compass needle swing. There is a parking lot on the Gunflint Trail at the far western end of this trail, but the trail may not be groomed all the way through. Ask locally about this trail; the Ham Lake Fire of 2007 burned right through here.

ASPEN ALLEY/RIVER TRAIL (3.2K)

Easier to intermediate/classical only. These two trails combine on either side of the Gunflint Trail for a relatively easy, open country loop. You can park off the road at the western end of the trails. The River Trail, on the north side, is better suited for more experienced skiers, running up and down an esker beside scenic Cross River. There are few aspens standing in Aspen Alley, but you get a great view of the hillside where they were all blown down in 1999.

Corridor Trail

WEST END TRAIL (6.5K)

Intermediate to advanced/classical and skating. Think of this trail as the big freeway connecting all destinations. It connects the River Trail on the west with Loon Lake on the east. Along the way the trail is hilly and challenging, with some very steep climbs and descents, dramatic views and intimate forests. The eastern half was mostly untouched by the blowdown.

Gunflint Lodge and Gunflint Pines trails

BIG PINE (3.2K)

Easier to Intermediate/classical only. Climb a steep hill from Gunflint Lodge on a broad trail through blowdown, then everything changes into a magic grotto of deep green forest ringed by dramatic steep cliffs. Dramatic scenery and signs of wildlife make this loop a great introduction to skiing Gunflint-style.

LITTLE PINE (2K)

Easier to intermediate/classical only. This is a small loop trail between Gunflint Lodge and Gunflint Pines. It winds through barns and access roads, all in blowdown areas.

RABBIT RUN (5.6K)

Easier to Intermediate/classical and skating. Branching off the West End Trail, this double-tracked trail runs along the bottom of a glacial ridge, past a luxury trailside shelter, then crosses the Gunflint, and parallels the Highlands Trail below the 140-foot cliff. The shelter is worth planning your day around, set between a cliff and a spruce bog, with propane heat, an indoor picnic table, even a rack to prop up your skis.

OVERLOOK (0.8K)

Easier to Intermediate/classical and skating. This short, hilly, double-tracked trail is your access to not only the scenic overlook but all the trails on the south side of the Gunflint Trail.

There's no real view at the overlook, but keep climbing on the trail to the Highlands Trail, over 300 feet up from the lodges, and you'll find a huge view of the lakes below through extensive blowdown areas.

SOUTH RIM (4.8K)

Intermediate to advanced/ classical only. Scoot along the top of a ridge with dramatic views of Gunflint Lake 400 feet below and the Canadian hills beyond. You could use the Lonely Lake Trail as part of a round trip back. Steep hills at both ends keep this section in the advanced category. Not recommended for low-snow conditions.

LONELY LAKE (4.8K)

Easier to Intermediate/ classical only. This double-tracked trail runs parallel to the South Rim Trail, but far below, beside pretty cliffs. The climb up at the eastern end from Heston's Lodge is particularly dramatic, with old-growth white pines and nice views of Gunflint Lake. A luxury warming hut is located near the west end of the trail.

UPPER GUNFLINT LODGING

The lodges on Gunflint Lake all provide excellent accommodations for skiers.

Moosehorn Lodge
196 N. Gunflint Lake Road, Grand Marais MN 55604, (218) 388-2233 or (888) 238-5975. www.moosehorn.com

Gunflint Lodge
143 S. Gunflint Lake Road, Grand Marais MN 55604, (218) 388-2294 or (800) 328-3325. www.gunflint.com

Gunflint Pines Resort
217 S. Gunflint Lake Road, Grand Marais MN 55604, (218) 388-4454 or (800) 533-5814. www.gunflintpines.com

Heston's Lodge
579 S. Gunflint Lake Road, Grand Marais MN 55604, (218) 388-2243 or (800) 338-7230. www.hestons.com

AMPERAGE WAY (4.5K)

Intermediate/classical and skating. Probably the best skating trail in the system. This trail parallels Lonely Lake Trail. Groomed eight-feet wide, it's meant for skaters and skijorers. The trail goes through a deep, thick cedar swamp.

Trails south of the Gunflint Trail

HIGHLANDS TRAIL (6.5K)

Intermediate to advanced/classical and skating. Hills at both ends of this double-tracked trail bracket a high-country run with nice views all along. The preferred travel direction is from east to west, allowing you to pause for nice views as you climb from the scenic overlook on the Gunflint Trail and providing for the full experience of Wipeout Hill, an "S" curve with a drop of over 120 feet to the Cross River below.

HAM LAKE TRAIL (4.8K)

Easier to Intermediate/classical only. Take a detour from the Highlands Trail and get into some serious moose country. The gently rolling, double-tracked terrain is well suited for novice skiers, except they would have to get through some intense climbs to get there. Most of this trail was untouched by the blowdown, and includes beautiful stretches of jack pine. Another luxury warming hut will come in handy for a snack break. By the way, Ham Lake itself is down below the trail but never actually visible.

NORTH STAR (9.6K)

Intermediate/classical only. Diverse habitats marked this trail even before the blowdown, with forestry management areas, wetlands and dense forests. After a nice descent to a crossing of Ham Creek, it's mostly open country. Cross the Gunflint Trail at the eastern end.

Resources for Skiers

The North Shore is a full-service skiing destination. Cross country ski sales and rental are available, and restaurants, grocery stores, and lodging—from remote, rustic cabins to elegant urban hotels—can be found along the way. When you're planning ahead, here are contacts to help you find the best experience.

North Shore Chambers and Associations

- Visit Duluth, (800) 4-DULUTH, www.visitduluth.com

- Two Harbors Area Chamber of Commerce
  (800) 777-7384, www.twoharborschamber.com

- Lutsen Tofte Tourism Association
  (888) 61-NORTH, www.americasnorthcoast.org

- Grand Marais Area Tourism Association
  (888) 922-5000, www.grandmarais.com

- Gunflint Trail Association
  (800) 338-6932, www.gunflint-trail.com

Ski Conditions

- Skier-posted reports from around the region:
  www.skinnyski.com

- Skier-posted reports from Northwest Wisconsin:
  www.norwiski.com

- Conditions around Northeast Minnesota:
  www.trailconditions.tk

- Grand Marais area ski conditions: (800) 897-7669

- Duluth city park trails: (218) 730-4321

Ski Rentals and Equipment

- Ski Hut, 1032 E. Fourth St., Duluth MN, 724-8525
  www.theskihut.com

- Continental Ski and Board, 1305 E. First St., Duluth MN
  (218) 728-4466, www.continentalski.com

- Sawtooth Outfitters, 7213 W. Highway 61, Tofte MN
  (218) 663-7643, www.sawtoothoutfitters.com
  Note: Direct access to Sugarbush trails.

- Devils Track Nordic Ski Shop, 922 Gunflint Trail, Grand Marais MN, (218) 387-3373, www.devilstracknordic.com Note: Direct access to Pincushion Mountain trails.

These ski areas also rent skis for use on site:

- Spirit Mountain
- Snowflake Nordic
- Lutsen Mountains

Also, many lodges rent skis to their guests.

Road Conditions

- Minnesota: Dial 511 or visit www.511mn.org

- Wisconsin: (800) ROADWIS (762-3947) or www.dot.wisconsin.gov/roads

Acknowledgements

This book would not have been possible without the tireless work of the hundreds of winter recreation lovers who groom the trails in winter, clear and build them in the summer, and promote their use year-round.

Special thanks to Josh McIntyre of Brule River State Forest, Kelly Fleissner of the City of Duluth, John Paulson of Minnesota Power, Michael O'Phelan at Solbakken Resort and Cascade Lodge, Gary Hoeft at Tettegouche State Park, John Kron and his Two Harbors trail, Dave Williams of Bear Track Outfitting, Scott Beattie and Pincushion B&B, Jeff Lynch and the Sugarbush Trail Association, Steve Schug with Superior National Forest, Mark Wendt of National Forest Lodge, Lee Kerfoot from Gunflint Lodge, Dan Baumann from Golden Eagle Lodge, and Barb and Ted Young from the Banadad Trail for their extra time and help in researching this book.

Many thanks to Gail Trowbridge for her professional editing and proofreading support.

Gunflint Lodge was my base for exploring the Upper Gunflint Trails, and I want to thank them for their North Woods hospitality.

Hans Slade, at ten years old, is the ultimate intermediate skier. If he likes a trail, so do I. Noah Slade, at nine years old, helped me see these trails with a beginner's eye. Until you master the snowplow, hills are a whole lot steeper.

Sally Rauschenfels is the true genius of this book. It was her vision that created it and her motivation that has seen it through. I would have lost the trail long ago without her.

Andrew Slade
Duluth, Minnesota

Index

4th of July storm, 1999 blowdown 135, 139, 146, 148

A

Access Trail, *Lester-Amity* 47
Afterhours Ski Trail 15, 16, **31**
Agate Beach 95
alder 103
Amity Creek 118
Amperage Way, *Upper Gunflint* 149
Artist's Point 95
Aspen Alley, *Upper Gunflint* 146
Aspen Trail, *Afterhours Ski Trail* 33

B

B&B Loop, *Pincushion Mountain* 131
Bagley Nature Area 15, **52**
Bally Creek 15, 16, 114, **122**
Bally Creek Camp 124
Bally Creek Trails, *Bally Creek* 124
Balsam Corner, *Northwoods Ski Touring Trail* 82
Banadad Trail 15, 16, **140**
Banadad Trail lodging 142
Banks, Charlie 50, 64
Bardon Peak Loop, *Magney Ski Area* 37
Bean Lake 81, 82
Bean Lake Spur, *Northwoods Ski Touring Trail* 82
Bearskin Lodge 134, 135
Bearskin Lodge trails, *Central Gunflint* 135
Bear Chase Trail, *Jay Cooke State Park* 22
Bear Cub World Cup, *Central Gunflint* 135
Bear Paw trail, *Boulder Lake* 58
Bear Paw/Blue Ox trailhead, *Boulder Lake* 57

Bear Track Outfitting Company 122, 124
Beaver Pond Spur, *Deer Yard* 121
Beaver River 82
Biddle Boys Trail, *Bally Creek* 124
Big Pine trail, *Upper Gunflint* 147
Big Pine Corner Loop, *Northwoods Ski Touring Trail* 82
birch forest 30, 103
Birch Hill Loop, *Gooseberry Falls State Park* 76
birds on North Shore 121
Bluefin Grille 95
Blue Loop, *Pattison State Park* 30
Blue Ox trail, *Boulder Lake* 58
Blue Trail, *Superior Municipal Forest* 26
Boulder Lake 14, 15, 16, **57**
Boundary Country Trekking 140
Brer Rabbit Run, *Bally Creek* 123
Bridge Run, *Sugarbush Trail System* 97
Brimson, Minnesota trails 67
Britton Peak trailhead, *Sugarbush Trail System* 92, 96, 97
Brule, Wisconsin trails 31
Bryan's Loop, *Korkki Nordic Ski Center* 66
Bullwinkle Run, *Bally Creek* 124
BWCA 137, 140, 142

C

Campground trail, *Central Gunflint* 135
Campground Loop, *Gooseberry Falls State Park* 76
Campground Loop, *Spirit Mountain* 51
Canal Park 95
Canosia Wildlife Management Area Trail 15, **61**

Canyon Curves loop, *Pincushion Mountain* 131
Caribou Highlands 107
Caribou Trail 104
Caribou Trail Connector, *Solbakken Resort* 111
Carlton, Minnesota trails 20
Carlton Peak 95, 96
Cascade Lodge 14, 16, 112, **115**
Cascade River 114, 117
Cascade River State Park 15, 16, 95, **112**, 120, 125
CCC Trail, *Jay Cooke State Park* 23
Cedar Woods, *Cascade River State Park* 113
Center Fields Loop, *Gooseberry Falls State Park* 76
Central Gunflint 14, 15, 17, **134**
Central Gunflint lodging 135
Central Loops, *Flathorn-Gegoka* 89
Charlie Banks Trail, *Spirit Mountain* 51
Chester Bowl 40
Chester Park 16
chickadee 24
Circle Loop, *Canosia Wildlife Management Area Trail* 63
Classic Trail, *Afterhours Trail* 33
Clearwater Road 134
Continental Ski and Board 151
Cook County Road 7 122
Cook County Road 36 105, 106
Cook County Road 41 109
Cook County Road 45 119, 125
Cook County Road 46 146
Cook County Road 48 122
Corundum Mine Loop, *Split Rock Lighthouse State Park* 80
Croft Yurt 142
Cross Fox Trail, *Central Gunflint* 138
Cross River 146, 149
Cut Across Trail, *Upper Gunflint* 146

D
Dam Parking Lot trailhead, *Boulder Lake* 57
Day Hill Trail, *Split Rock Lighthouse State Park* 79
deer 110, 114, 125
Deer Track Loop, *Solbakken Resort* 10
Deer Yard 16, 112, 115, **119**
Deer Yard Lake 120
Deer Yard Loop, *Deer Yard* 121
Devil Track River 130
Devils Track Nordic Ski Shop 152
Dorothy's Loop, *Korkki Nordic Ski Center* 66
Duluth, Minnesota trails 35, 38, 40, 42, 45, 49, 52, 54, 57, 64
Duluth-Superior Area 18
Duluth city parks 37

E
Eagle Mountain 108, 124
Eastern Hills, *Gooseberry Falls State Park* 77
Eastern Loops, *Flathorn-Gegoka* 88
East Bay beach 95
East Loop, *Bagley Nature Area* 53
East Overlook Loop, *Pincushion Mountain* 130
Elbow Creek 133
Elys Peak Loop, *Magney Ski Area* 37
Entry Trail, *Afterhours Ski Trail* 33
Erik Judeen Trail, *Spirit Mountain* 51
Erkki Harju Ski Trail 72
Expert Loop, *Piedmont Ski Trail* 39

F
Fifth Falls, Gooseberry River 118
Fire Tower trail, *Deer Yard* 120
Flathorn-Gegoka 15, 56, **87**
Flathorn Lake 87, 88
Flour Lake 135, 137, 139
Forest Road 158 122
Forest Road 315 140
Forest Road 332 119

Fosseide, Pete 50

Full Loop, *Magney Ski Area* 36

G

George's Trail, *Snowflake Nordic Center* 56

George Hovland Trail, *Spirit Mountain* 51

George Washington Trail 15, **132**

Golden Eagle Lodge 134, 135

Golden Eagle Lodge area trails 137

Golf Course Loop, *Lester-Amity* 48

Golf Course Trail, *Lutsen Area* 105

Gooseberry Falls State Park 14, 16, 17, **74**, 95

Gooseberry River 76, 118

Gooseberry Trailside Suites 77

Grand Marais, Minnesota trails 122, 128, 132, 134, 140, 144

Grand Marais Area Tourism Association 151

Great Minnesota Ski Pass 11, 12

Greely Creek Trail, *Jay Cooke State Park* 23

Green Trails, *Superior Municipal Forest* 26

Gunflint Lake 148

Gunflint Lodge 144, 147, 148

Gunflint Pines Resort 147, 148

Gunflint Tavern 131

Gunflint Trail 15, 126

Gunflint Trail Association 151

H

Hall Loop, *Solbakken Resort* 111

Hall Road 109

Ham Creek 149

Ham Lake 149

Ham Lake Fire 143

Ham Lake Trail, *Upper Gunflint* 149

Hartley Field 15, **42**

Herringbone Hill, *Northwoods Ski Touring Trail* 82

Heston's Lodge 148

Highlands Trail, *Upper Gunflint* 149

High Trail, *Jay Cooke State Park* 22

Hilfiker Hill Loop, *Pincushion Mountain* 131

Hogback Loop, *Sugarbush Trail System* 97

Hogback Ridge 97

Homestead Acres trail, *Lutsen Area* 105

Homestead Loop, *Sugarbush Trail System* 97

Hovland, George 50, 54

I

Inner Loop, *Hartley Field* 44

Inner Loop, *Lester-Amity* 47

Inner Loops, *Mother Bear Ski Trail* 68

Inner Loops, *Sugarbush Trail System* 96

Inside Trail, *Erkki Harju Ski Trail* 73

Isabella, Minnesota trails 87

J

Jane's Trail, *Snowflake Nordic Center* 56

Jay Cooke State Park 15, 16, **20**

Johnson Heritage Post 131

Joynes Ben Franklin Department Store 131

Judeen, Erik 50

K

Kadunce River 118

Kimball's Bay 27

Knife River, Minnesota 118

Korkki Nordic Ski Center 10, 14, 16, 17, **64**

L

Lace Lake trail, *Banadad Trail* 143

lake–effect snow 10, 31, 87, 89

Lakes and Hills trail, *Tettegouche State Park* 86

Lakeview National Golf Course 73

Lakewalk 95
Lake County 70
Lake Gegoka 87
Lake Superior ice 80
Larry Sorenson Trail, *Spirit Mountain* 51
Laurentian Divide 142
Lester-Amity 16, **45**
Lester River 118
Leveaux Overlook trail, *Sugarbush Trail System* 101
Lima Grade 140
Little Devil Track River 131
Little Isabella River 88
Little Joe Trail, *Afterhours Ski Trail* 34
Little Ollie cabin 142
Little Ollie Road 140
Little Pine trail, *Upper Gunflint* 147
Little Two Harbors Trail, *Split Rock Lighthouse State Park* 79
Lonely Lake trail, *Upper Gunflint* 148
Lonesome Grouse trail, *Boulder Lake* 60
Lookout Mountain 114, 117
Lookout Mountain trail, *Cascade Lodge* 117
Loon Lake 147
Loon Lake boat access 140, 144
Loop Trail, *Afterhours Ski Trail* 34
Lower Lake Trail, *Jay Cooke State Park* 22
Lower Loop, *Tettegouche State Park* 86
Lower Ridge Run, *Cascade Lodge* 117
Lower Snowman trail, *Pincushion Mountain* 131
Lutsen, Minnesota trails 104, 106, 109, 112, 115, 119
Lutsen Area 104
Lutsen Connector, *Cascade Lodge* 118

Lutsen Connector, *Sugarbush Trail System* 102
Lutsen Mountain 106
Lutsen Mountains Nordic Center 106
Lutsen Mountain lodging 107
Lutsen Resort 105, 108
Lutsen Scientific and Natural Area 105
Lutsen Sea Villas 102
Lutsen Tofte Tourism Association 102, 151

M
Magnetic Rock trail, *Upper Gunflint* 146
Magney Ski Area 15, **35**
Main Loop, *Chester Bowl* 41
Main Loop, *George Washington Trail* 133
Main Loop, *Piedmont Ski Trail* 39
Maple Corner Loops, *Northwoods Ski Touring Trail* 82
Maple Loop, *Sugarbush Trail System* 98
Maple Trail, *Afterhours Ski Trail* 33
Massie Loop, *Solbakken Resort* 111
Meadows Loop, *Solbakken Resort* 111
Merrill Logging Loop, *Split Rock Lighthouse State Park* 80
Mic Mac Lake 86
Minnesota Power 57
Minnesota state ski pass 11
moose 99, 108, 125, 139, 149
Moosehorn Lodge 148
Moosehorn Lodge trails 146
Moose Area Loop, *Bally Creek* 124
Moose Fence trailhead, *Sugarbush Trail System* 92, 98, 99
Moose Mountain 105, 114
Moose Mountain Trails, *Cascade River State Park* 114
Moose Ridge trail, *Central Gunflint* 138

Mother Bear Ski Trail 67
Murmur Road 119
Mystery Mountain 106, 108
Mystery Mountain, *Lutsen Mountains Nordic Center* 107

N

National Forest Lodge 87, 89
Nelson, Carl Axel 108
Nine Pine trail, *Boulder Lake* 60
Nipisiquit Lake 86
norpine skiing 16, 95, 99, 106, 111
North-South Link, *Central Gunflint* 137
Northern Loops, *Flathorn-Gegoka* 89
Northwoods Ski Touring Trail 15, 81
North Advanced Loop, *Pincushion Mountain* 130
North Flour Loops, *Central Gunflint* 138
North Parking Lot trailhead, *Boulder Lake* 57
North Shore Mountains 90
North Star trail, *Upper Gunflint* 149
North Superior Ski and Run Club 128

O

Oak Trail, *Afterhours Ski Trail* 33
Oak Trail, *Jay Cooke State Park* 24
Oberg Mountain Trail, *Sugarbush Trail System* 101
Old Logging Camp, *Central Gunflint* 137, 138
Ole Hyvaa Loop, *Pincushion Mountain* 131
Onion River Road, *Sugarbush Trail System* 101
Onion River Road trailhead, *Sugarbush Trail System* 92, 99, 100
Orange Loop, *Pattison State Park* 30

Otter Run trail, *Boulder Lake* 58
Outer Loop, *Hartley Field* 44
Outside Trail, *Erkki Harju Ski Trail* 73
Overlook trail, *Upper Gunflint* 147
Overlook Loops, *Mother Bear Ski Trail* 69
Overlook Loops, *Pincushion Mountain* 130
Overlook Trail, *Canosia Wildlife Management Area Trail* 63
Ox Cart Trail, *Central Gunflint* 135

P

Pattison State Park 16, 28
Pete Fosseide Trail, *Spirit Mountain* 51
Picnic Loop, *Sugarbush Trail System* 97
Piedmont Ski Trail 16, 38
Pike Lake Road 119
Pincushion Bed & Breakfast 128, 130
Pincushion Mountain 14, 15, 16, 128
Pincushion Mountain Loop, *Pincushion Mountain* 130
Pisten-Bully groomer 90, 115, 126
Pokegama Bay 27
Poplar Corner trail, *Northwoods Ski Touring Trail* 82
Poplar Creek 143
Poplar Creek trail, *Central Gunflint* 137
Poplar Creek Guesthouse B&B 140, 142
Poplar River 105
Power Line trail, *Upper Gunflint* 146
Purple Trail, *Superior Municipal Forest* 26

R

Rabbit Run trail, *Upper Gunflint* 147

Red Loop, *Pattison State Park* 30
Red Pine Loops, *Central Gunflint* 138
red squirrel 60
Red Trails, *Superior Municipal Forest* 26
resources for skiers 150
Rib Lake Road 140
Ridge Runner trail, *Boulder Lake* 58
Ridge Trails, *Jay Cooke State Park* 22
River Trail, *Afterhours Ski Trail* 33
River Trail, *Upper Gunflint* 146
River Trails, *Cascade Lodge* 116
road conditions 152
Rolling Pin trail, *Boulder Lake* 58
Rollins Creek trail, *Sugarbush Trail System* 102
Ruby Lake 139
Rudy Lake 137, 139

S
Sawbill Trail 92, 97
Sawtooth Outfitters 151
Shoreline Trail, *Cascade River State Park* 113
Short Loop trail, *Deer Yard* 121
Shovel Point 95
Silver Bay, Minnesota trails 81, 84
Silver Creek Trail, *Jay Cooke State Park* 22
Sivertson Gallery 131
Sixmile Creek valley 99
Sixmile Crossing trail *Sugarbush Trail System* 99
Skating Road, *Bally Creek* 124
ski conditions 151
Ski Hill Road 104, 105, 106
Ski Hut 151
ski rentals and equipment 151
ski wax 17, 48
Smokey Creek 82
snacks 34, 48
snowbelt 31, 89

Snowflake Nordic Center 14, 15, 16, **54**
snowshoe hare 60, 67
Solbakken Resort 14, 105, **109**, 111, 118
South Loop, *Mother Bear Ski Trail* 68
South Rim trail, *Upper Gunflint* 148
Spirit Mountain 14, 16, **49**
Spirit Mountain Villas 51
Split Rock Creek 80
Split Rock Lighthouse State Park 16, **78**
Split Rock River 118
Spruce Corner trail, *Northwoods Ski Touring Trail* 82
Spruce Creek Connector Trail, *Solbakken Resort* 111
spruce forest 33, 99, 103
Spruce Trail, *Afterhours Ski Trail* 33
Spruce Trail, *Jay Cooke State Park* 22
Stoney Point 95
storm watching 95
Sucker River 118
Sugarbush Trail Association 101
Sugarbush Trail System 14, 15, 16, 17, **92**
sugar maple forest 103
Summer Home Road, *Central Gunflint* 135
Summit View trail, *Sugarbush Trail System* 94
Sundling Creek Loop, *Bally Creek* 123
Superior, Wisconsin trails 25, 28
Superior Hiking Trail 86, 94, 117, 130, 131
Superior Municipal Forest 15, 16, **25**
Superior National Forest, Gunflint Ranger District 132
Superior National golf course 102, 104, 105

T

Tall Pines Yurt 142
Tettegouche Camp 82, 84
Tettegouche Connector, *Northwoods Ski Touring Trail* 82
Tettegouche Lake 86
Tettegouche State Park 15, 17, **84**, 95
The 6K, *Korkki Nordic Ski Center* 65
Thomson Trail, *Jay Cooke State Park* 23
Timber Cruiser trail, *Boulder Lake* 58
Tim Knapp Trail, *Banadad Trail* 143
Tofte, Minnesota trails 92
Tofte trailhead, *Sugarbush Trail System* 92, **94**
Town of Canosia, Minnesota trails 61
tracks (animal) 60, 69, 125
Trapper Pass 105
Triangle Trails, *Jay Cooke State Park* 24
Two Harbors, Minnesota trails 72, 74, 78
Two Harbors Area Chamber of Commerce 151
Two Harbors Ski Rec Trail 72

U

Ullr Mountain trail, *Lutsen Mountains Nordic Center* 107
Upland Loop, *Sugarbush Trail System* 98, 99
Upper Gunflint 14, 15, 17, **144**
Upper Gunflint lodging 148
Upper Lake Trail, *Jay Cooke State Park* 22
Upper Loops, *Lester-Amity* 47
Upper Ridge Run, *Cascade Lodge* 117
Upper Snowman trail, *Pincushion Mountain* 131

V

Valley Trails, *Gooseberry Falls State Park* 77
Visit Duluth 151

W

warmer by the lake 15, 77
Warrens Road trail, *Upper Gunflint* 146
weasels 69
weather, North Shore 10, 63
Western Loop, *Cascade Lodge* 117
West End Trail, *Upper Gunflint* 147
West Loop, *Bagley Nature Area* 53
West Overlook Loop, *Pincushion Mountain* 130
Whitesides Loop, *Solbakken Resort* 110
White Pine Trail, *Afterhours Ski Trail* 34
White Pine Trail, *Jay Cooke State Park* 23
wolf kill 125
Wolf Pack Run, *Bally Creek* 125
Wolf Point trail, *Central Gunflint* 137
Wood Duck Loop, *Sugarbush Trail System* 96

Y

yellow birch 103
Yellow Loop, *Superior Municipal Forest* 26
Young, Ted & Barb 143
yurt 140, 142